American Federalism:
A New Partnership
for the Republic

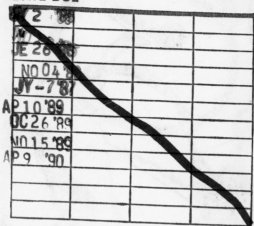

AMERICAN FEDERALISM: A NEW PARTNERSHIP FOR THE REPUBLIC

Robert B. Hawkins, Jr., *Editor*
Lamar Alexander
Benjamin L. Cardin
Albert J. Davis
Eugene Eidenberg
Daniel J. Elazar
Alan F. Holmer
A. E. Dick Howard
Michael S. Joyce
Paul Laxalt
John McClaughry
W. S. Moore
E. S. Savas
William A. Schambra
Stephen L. Schechter
Wm. Craig Stubblebine
David B. Swoap
Murray L. Weidenbaum
F. Clifton White
Aaron Wildavsky
Richard S. Williamson

Institute for Contemporary Studies
San Francisco, California

Distributed by Transaction Books
New Brunswick (USA) and London (UK)

Inquiries, book orders, and catalog requests should be addressed to
the Institute for Contemporary Studies, Suite 811, 260 California
Street, San Francisco, California 94111—415—398—3010.

Library of Congress Catalog No. 82—80329.

Library of Congress Cataloging in Publication Data
Main entry under title:

American federalism, a new partnership for the
      Republic.

      Includes the proceedings of a special conference
on federalism held in Washington, D.C., Sept. 1981.
      Bibliography: p.
      Includes index.
      1. Federal government—United States—Congresses.
2. Intergovernmental fiscal relations—United States
—Congresses. 3. United States—Politics and
government—1981-   —Congresses. I. Hawkins,
Robert B. II. Alexander, Lamar. III. Institute for
Contemporary Studies.
JK325.A656 1982   321.02'0973   82—14040
      ISBN 0—917616—50—2

CONTENTS

I

Introduction

II

Foundations of Federalism

III

The Reagan Administration's Federalism Policy Proposals

vi

VII

Conclusion

CONTRIBUTORS

LAMAR ALEXANDER
Governor of Tennessee

BENJAMIN L. CARDIN
Speaker, Maryland House of Delegates;
chairman, Ways and Means Committee

ALBERT J. DAVIS
Senior analyst, Taxation and Finance staff,
Advisory Commission on Intergovernmental Relations

EUGENE EIDENBERG
Director, Democratic National Committee

DANIEL J. ELAZAR
Director, Center for the Study of Federalism;
professor of political science, Temple University

ROBERT B. HAWKINS, Jr.
President, The Sequoia Institute

ALAN F. HOLMER
Deputy assistant to the president for intergovernmental affairs

A. E. DICK HOWARD
White Burkett Miller Professor of Law and Public Affairs,
University of Virginia

MICHAEL S. JOYCE
Executive director, John M. Olin Foundation

PAUL LAXALT
U.S. senator (R), Nevada

JOHN McCLAUGHRY
Senior policy adviser, Office of Policy Development

W. S. MOORE
Director of legal policy studies, American Enterprise Institute

E. S. SAVAS
Assistant secretary for policy development and research,
Department of Housing and Urban Development

WILLIAM A. SCHAMBRA
Assistant director of constitutional studies,
American Enterprise Institute

STEPHEN L. SCHECHTER
Associate professor of political science, Russell Sage College;
fellow, Center for the Study of Federalism, Temple University

WM. CRAIG STUBBLEBINE
Von Tobel Professor of Political Science;
director, Center for the Study of Law Structures,
Claremont McKenna College and Graduate School

DAVID B. SWOAP
Under secretary, Department of Health and Human Services

MURRAY L. WEIDENBAUM
Chairman, Council of Economic Advisers

F. CLIFTON WHITE
President, F. Clifton White and Associates, Inc.

AARON WILDAVSKY
Professor of political science, University of California, Berkeley

RICHARD S. WILLIAMSON
Assistant to the president for intergovernmental affairs

PREFACE

Until recently, concerns about the state and health of the American federal system seemed very close to a joke frequently told about the weather: everybody talks about it, but nobody ever does anything about it. President Reagan's proposal to move $47 billion in public spending among the federal, state, and local governments marks a sharp departure from the past tendency toward inaction; and the public debate about how functions and responsibilities should be distributed among levels of government and the private sector is once again intensely joined.

In September 1981 the Institute for Contemporary Studies held a special conference in Washington, D.C., on the subject of federalism. Organized by Robert B. Hawkins, Jr., of the Sequoia Institute, with help from Daniel J. Elazar, of the Center for the Study of Federalism, the conference focused on issues that were preoccupying the Reagan administration in this area, which the administration has identified as one of its major policy concerns. Besides scholars concentrating in this field, we had a number of participants from the Washington policy community—including the White House—as well as representatives from state and local governments.

Most of the chapters that follow are taken from papers given at the conference, together with comments by respondents. After the conference, however, we commissioned additional papers from Albert J. Davis and Michael S. Joyce, and we are also reprinting William A. Schambra's analysis of the theoretical roots of federalism.

In these days of broad reexamination of traditional responsibilities of government, institutional issues of federalism are
often at the center of debates on how to resolve problems related to severe constraints in public budgets. Many of the
issues considered in this book focus on the dominant themes
and most basic concerns related to the kind of society we
want to live in. There is a feeling among many specialists in
this area that issues of federalism have not received the attention and consideration that their importance merits. The
spirited reactions to the president's proposals suggest that
this may be changing. This book should help clarify many of
the underlying issues involved and thus encourage a more informed debate.

A. Lawrence Chickering
Executive Director
Institute for Contemporary Studies

San Francisco, California
August 1983

I

Introduction

1

ROBERT B. HAWKINS, Jr.

American Federalism: Again at the Crossroads

Nationalism and managerialism. Reactions to central-ized benevolence. Limiting federal activities. "Iron triangles." Public goods and economic externalities. Alternative strategies for reform.

Federalism is again an issue of public interest and debate, and the debate promises to be intense. President Reagan's philosophic commitment to restore federalism to its "first principles"—combined with his sweeping policy initia-tives—is likely to keep federalism on the political front

burner for some time to come. Unlike past presidential
efforts to reform the federal system, Reagan federalism is
unlikely to be soon eclipsed by other issues of national or international scope.

Any time that $47 billion changes locations in govern-
ment, there will be potential big winners and big losers, and
the potential losers can be expected to organize in opposition
to the change. Special interest groups will thus constitute the
first—and possibly the noisiest—participants in the coming
federalism debate. The president's proposal to place Medicare completely in the hands of the federal government, and
to place welfare and food stamps in the hands of the states,
involves a huge shift of resources. Health providers, national
corporations, welfare recipients, and state and local governments all have a great stake in the outcome. And if this is not
enough to give the debate intensity, one merely has to add
the effects of the sagging economy on revenues of state and
local governments.

Yet the debate over federalism will involve more than the
pleadings of special interest groups. Reagan federalism will
also have to face criticism on intellectual and ideological
grounds. Establishment liberals will make the time-worn
argument that "federalism" is nothing more than a code
word for "states' rights"—a means of tearing down social
welfare programs, a way for the federal government to back
off from its commitment to civil rights and equations of
equity. But there will also be criticism from the conservative
side. In the minds of some intellectuals, the administration's
failure to articulate precisely the first principles of federalism, which the president so often invokes, will lead to a con-
viction that the New Federalism is little more than a reprise
of the old, merely administrative federalism of the Nixon era.
A more fundamental criticism from this quarter is that
Reagan federalism has so far failed to directly address the
constitutional issues at stake, has tended to ignore the
necessity for a rebuilding of political parties at the state and

local levels, and has neglected to address social problems from a consistently federalist perspective. Conservatives with a nationalistic perspective tend to see the current hegemony of the Republican party mainly as an opportunity to implement their agenda on a national level. Abortion is a good example of an issue in which federalist and nationalist approaches can be at odds. The Reagan administration might well support the Hatch amendment on abortion, which would take the issue out of the national arena and leave it up to the states. Obviously such a move would not be in keeping with the desire of some conservatives for a national resolution of the issue in their favor. Just as important, many conservatives regard the federal takeover of Medicaid as a dangerous first step toward nationalized medicine.

FEDERALISM AS AN ISSUE

The last six presidents have all raised the issue of federalism in some manner. Yet in each case it has rapidly faded as a driving issue on the national agenda. One reason for this is that federalism has not been a topic of real intellectual interest for the last seventy years. Many intellectuals have argued that it is an archaic form of government, a remnant of the horse and buggy days of American civilization, a system that should be replaced by a national form of government.

Historical trends have reinforced this critique of American federalism. The emergence of a strong national government during the depression—accelerated by World War II and reinforced not only by the Great Society but also by the "New Federalism" of the Nixon administration—focused the eyes of state and local policymakers on Washington. One does not need detailed historical knowledge to perceive the general direction of this development. One merely has to recall the heady days of the Great Society to remember that there was a time when business leaders and local state officials could hardly conceive of solving problems without some type of comprehensive program from Washington. Civil rights, urban renewal, and the eradication of poverty all required a national framework and national dollars for their solutions.

Even before the New Deal came along, it is fair to say that many Americans had become mesmerized by the ideas of nationalism and managerialism. Reformers, both academic and practical, helped create the myth that large-scale organizations, hierarchically structured and responsible to a single center of power, were indispensable to solving problems. Mimicking the vaunted "efficiency" of gigantic business corporations, reformers over the years instituted a host of changes from which no sector of our civil society has been immune. Schools, local governments, and even state governments have been reshaped under the force of this program; consolidation of power and authority has been the constant theme song of those seeking modern governmental institutions for an "interdependent" and "modern" society.

Unfortunately for reformers, myths have a way of being mugged by reality. The promises of efficiency and responsiveness from centralized institutions have been far from realized. In fact, many reformers have been startled by reactions of recipients of centralized benevolence. As educational systems have become centralized—breaking the important civil nexus between family, community, and school—we have seen a steady decrease in citizen support for public education. As authority over school decisions has been centralized by state departments of education and by activist judges, we have seen a corresponding erosion of legitimacy in the public schools.

We can see the same phenomena in poor and middle-class urban neighborhoods. After repeated and largely unsuccessful national attempts to revitalize, renew, and develop declining cities, we find today a new answer to urban problems in the form of a rebirth of local and voluntary efforts to provide for the safety and the orderly development of many urban neighborhoods. It is not uncommon today to find voluntary block organizations in large cities providing services either through citizens' efforts or through voluntary assessments for the provision of added security, playground maintenance, or block improvements.

Although schools and neighborhoods do not always figure prominently in the national debate on federalism, they actually provide the clearest picture of the fundamental issues and problems federalism raises. In both realms, we see serious instances of institutional failure—failure of public institutions to sustain a set of political decisions that maintains legitimacy, consensus among citizens, and hence political authority.

The Founding Fathers dealt with similar issues of institutional failure. The failure of the Articles of Confederation to sustain a viable national government capable of providing for the national defense and of sustaining the emergence of a commercial nation was a real sign of institutional weaknesses. In the modern idiom of management, we can say the Founding Fathers dealt with the problem of assessing the capabilities and limitations of different governmental arrangements. Uppermost in their minds was the problem of creating a national government that was capable of energetic action—yet within clear political bounds. The Framers held that to invest all power in a national government was the very definition of tyranny, and that such a political arrangement would enervate state and local effort. Consequently, they limited national authority through a system of checks and balances. The drafting and ratification of the Constitution was a political act designed to develop consensus on the fundamental rules by which the American society would govern itself. In the process of shaping the Constitution, the Founding Fathers created one of the most successful experiments in self-governance—perhaps the only really complete one. For this reason alone federalism is essential.

But today we see a different kind of debate. Today's debate is not focused on the Constitution of our government and on how it might be changed to deal with such problems as excessive spending or overcentralization of power in Washington. Rather, the current debate has been narrowed to a merely technical and managerial issue: what functions should go to what units of government with what tax resources? Politically, this narrowing of concerns may be the only avenue open to the administration, but it is not without perils. For the narrowing of the question obfuscates many of the real issues of federalism and could even cost the president any meaningful reform of the federal system.

FEDERALISM AND "BIG GOVERNMENT"

It is in the context of this current debate that the concern with federalism dovetails with the critique of "big government." Indeed, the recollection of federalist "first principles" is a valuable, and arguably natural, response to the central government's long record of failures in the recent past. Time and again during the past thirty years, federal programs designed to achieve salutary purposes have worked deleterious effects, and the federal government's "solutions" have resulted only in new problems. On most of these government efforts the verdict is pretty clear. Studies of economic regulation indicate that such regulation has increased the costs of services, skewed the rational investment of resources, and inadvertently favored the interests of one group at the expense of another. In a similar way, programs of social regulation and welfare have promoted dependency where they sought to encourage independence, while simultaneously feeding the growth of a bureaucracy increasingly accountable to no one. This is not to argue that there are no functions for the federal government to assume. Nonetheless, these misgivings about the power of central government are by no means confined to conservatives. A former Democratic director of the Office of Management and Budget has similarly contended that there are very real organizational limits to federal activities and that these limits have already been exceeded.

This persistent and sustained institutional failure at the federal level has led us to contemplate turning such functions over either to the private sector or to state and local governments. In the contemplation of such a change, an understanding of federalism is crucial, because federalist first principles define the types of authority that state and local governments would need in order to overcome the institutional failures that have been experienced in the federal sphere. Should the role of the states be merely administrative, should they be equal partners, or should they have sole discretion?

A parallel set of difficulties and questions arises in the realm of taxing and spending. The economic ill effects of excessive federal spending, federal deficits, and off-budget borrowing have prompted a reexamination of the institutional incentives responsible for what now appear to be persistent defects. Federalist principles again provide a framework for grasping and solving these problems. From a federalist perspective, it can be argued that the increased dependence of state and local governments on federal funds has undermined traditional checks on spending built into the federal system. State and local governments, once perceived as countervailing powers to federal authority, have become potent lobbies for increases in federal spending. At the same time, groups that traditionally solved their problems through local or state governments have increasingly turned to the federal government for aid and redress. This convergence of interest groups on Washington has contributed to the emergence of what policymakers now describe as "iron triangles" of interest, composed of interest groups, congres-

sional committees, and federal bureaucracies. These iron
triangles have created a framework that all but ensures an
ineluctible growth in spending at the federal level.

Federalism provides one—and really the only—means of
reversing this tendency. To reduce the growth of government, it is necessary to return clear authority, both political
and fiscal, to state and local governments. For only when the
political pressure is taken off Congress can we expect to see
authentic attempts to balance the budget and cut back
federal programs.

Federalism, as conceived by the Reagan administration, is
a necessary—though not sufficient—condition to bring
about these desired changes. To succeed decisively in this
effort to reduce political pressure on the federal government,
we must also address the question of how we can again inte-
grate political authority into community. We must ask ourselves how communities of human scale, in a mobile society,
might have limited yet real political authority. For unless
there are mediating structures through which citizens can
create and sustain a sense of community, we will see the continual escalation of demands on government—an escalation
that leads invariably to Washington, D.C. This last issue
may, in fact, be the most important in any consideration of
federalism. Unless citizens have the opportunity to solve
problems within their own communities—an opportunity
that centralized systems have largely destroyed—there is
little reason to think that merely sending programs back to
state and local governments will have much real impact.

FEDERALISM AS "MANAGEMENT" OR POLITICS

Let us return to the managerial question of assessing the
capabilities and limitations of governmental arrangements,

for the heart of the issue is to be found in how we understand this question. The modern answer to the problem of democratic government is to be found in the liberal bias in favor of the nation-state—a bias supported by a certain body of economic and administrative theory. In the modern liberal view, government is said to be concerned with two categories of things: public goods and economic externalities. Public goods are understood to be goods that by nature are not divisible, and consequently goods that government cannot prevent citizens from consuming. National defense is the paramount example of a public good: citizens cannot purchase more or less national defense individually. National defense for one citizen is national defense for all. But people vary in their classification of particular goods as public or private. Some people argue that economic policy can be considered a public good in the same sense as national defense, because the net effect of economic policy—the good or ill health of the economy as a whole—is felt by all citizens. There are those who would even classify education as a public good under the same definition. In addition to its concern with the provision of public goods, government in this view is assigned the role of alleviating the negative external effects of economic activities. Pollution is an example of an economic externality that has been used to justify government intervention and centralization of power. As Daniel Elazar points out in this volume, the idea of efficient administration through hierarchical structures has gone hand in hand with the economic concepts of public goods and market externalities. Both concepts have provided a strong impetus for the growth of central government and centralized management on all levels of society.

Apart from the fact, as we have said, that these centralized, hierarchical structures have frequently failed to achieve the responsiveness or efficiencies of scale that advocates have attributed to them, they raise a fundamental difficulty that goes to the heart of federalism. In the process of rearranging things, reformers have ignored the crucial relationship between community and political authority. The evidence is now mounting that as authority has been centralized—i.e., taken away from citizens and local communities—legitimacy and social connectedness have also been lost. Nowhere is this more apparent than in our ravaged neighborhoods and schools. Over a century ago, Alexis de Tocqueville predicted the enervating effect that centralization would have on local political activity. He also emphasized the beneficial results that decentralization of authority might have on political legitimacy. *E pluribus unum*, "one out of many," expressed—and still expresses—a basic tenet of American society and politics. Federalism, as a partnership and as the dispersion of political authority to a number of semi-independent centers, implies that Americans can belong to a number of important communities. In fact, these notions, when coupled with the Constitution, provide the general framework within which citizens can retain strong commitments to a national government while still having strong bonds to their neighborhoods, schools, and local governments. A blind faith in the nation-state and in the power of management has led us to ignore these important bonds between local communities and political authority, with high costs.

The integration, both formal and informal, of political authority into community has been one of the fundamental hallmarks of American federalism. There was a time when modern notions of mass society, management, and rational planning might have been seen as an epitaph for federalism, but the American public has in recent years confounded the experts. The reemergence of interest in communities and the deep-seated feelings for belonging to them are again forces in American life. In fact, as one listened to Ronald Reagan's acceptance speech at the Republican national convention, one was struck by the number of community chords it sounded.

What is indeed ironic is that while President Reagan realizes that we must return to the first principles of federalism, his hands are tied with regard to the practical ways in which this can be accomplished. If the Reagan administration could take unilateral actions to reform the federal system, there would, in fact, be no federal system to reform. The only real course of action open to the president is the one that he has chosen. By sending functions and tax resources back to the states, he has taken the necessary first step. The second step necessary—so far not talked about—is to refashion the political relationships within states; for just as federalism determines the relationship between the national government and the states, so the principle must be extended to structure relationships between state and local governments. Strained relationships between many states and their local governments—a mistrust created largely by the rush to consume federal dollars and programs—must be overcome by the participants themselves. To ask the federal government to do the restructuring is to fall back into the old perspective of seeking a centralized solution to what is in fact a constitutional problem that obtains between state and local governments.

PROSPECTS FOR REFORM

Fundamental reform of the federal system is long overdue. After decades of national-level solutions and improvements in management, we are now ready for a fundamental debate on principles that structure our political institutions. President Reagan has framed the issue in ways that his predecessors failed to do. There is none of the paternalism of the Johnson years, nor any of the aggressive and coercive tone of the Nixon years. What has been offered is an opportunity for real political change, for a realignment of political authority in our society. However, there are a number of difficult roadblocks that must be overcome if there is to be real change.

The initial concept of trading functions and tax bases is a good first step. However, it may well prove to be inadequate, requiring the administration to broaden the issue and change direction. Part of the problem will be in building a coalition. This may be difficult to do, given the hostility between state and local governments and the wariness that many business groups may feel toward having to deal with fifty states instead of one federal agency. Likewise, in an election year with a slow economy, the federalism initiatives are likely to suffer at the hands of political expediency. Finally, the administration will face congressional resistance—for reasons of power, ideology, or pride—to relinquishing prerogatives that will be handed over to state and local governments.

An alternative strategy for the administration would have two prongs. First, it might give serious consideration to the balanced budget amendment presently making its way through the U.S. Senate. Such an amendment has many attractive qualities. First and foremost, it does not immediately threaten important constituents of the president's economic coalition, particularly business. Second, it would not only decrease the rate of growth of federal expenditures but would also force Congress to look at the real opportunity costs of competing programs, forcing many programs back to the states. Third, thirty state legislatures have already passed resolutions calling for such an amendment, which provides a ready base of consensus for its eventual passage. Finally, the amendment process, especially in the states, would build the type of consensus needed to sustain real change in federal-state relationships over the long term and would put in place strong incentives for fiscal constraint, incentives that would last long past the Reagan years.

The second prong of an alternative strategy would be for the president and his administration to begin to articulate a new public philosophy supportive of community. Family, voluntary associations, neighborhoods, schools, and local

governments are all issues tied into federalism. Their connection to federalism should be clearly articulated. By force-
fully addressing these issues, the president might well start a
realignment of the federal system that even Congress will
not be able to ignore.

II

Foundations of
Federalism

2

WILLIAM A. SCHAMBRA

The Roots of the American Public Philosophy*

The Federalists and popular government. Property, diversity, self-interest, and inequality. The Anti-Federalists: a homogeneous citizenry. Wealth and U.S. traditions. Liberalism and utopia.

Is the New Deal public philosophy dead? Has a new public philosophy arisen to take its place since the 1980 election? We may not be able to answer these questions for many

*Reprinted with permission of the author from *The Public Interest*, No. 67 (Spring 1982), pp. 36−48; © by National Affairs, Inc.

years, of course, but there is no denying that a major shift in
the terms of political discourse has occurred in Washington,
whether temporarily or permanently. We no longer ask ourselves *the* question that dominated domestic national politics
for fifty years, through Democratic and Republican administrations alike: what major new programs should the federal
government undertake in order to bring about a more equitable distribution of resources in America? Beneath this
change there seems to be a general disenchantment with the
image of America as a great national community—a "Great
Society"—bound together by a powerful central government. Instead, we ask ourselves today how we can shore up
the "small societies"—state and local governments and private associations—and how they can be brought to assume
many of the burdens heretofore borne by the federal government. And today we ask ourselves how we may re-stimulate
the production of resources in America, rather than how we
may insure that resources are equally distributed.

Whether this shift of concerns turns out to be temporary
or permanent, we cannot understand the new terms of political discourse—or the old ones—until we understand the
two American political traditions that they reflect.

THE FEDERALISTS

Two traditions of American political thought grew out of a
quarrel at the time of the Founding in 1787. The Federalists,
led by Alexander Hamilton and James Madison, and the
Anti-Federalists, including such people as Patrick Henry,
Richard Henry Lee, Mercy Warren, and Melancton Smith,
disagreed about how best to constitute popular government.
Madison and Hamilton—principal authors of *The Federalist*
essays defending the proposed Constitution—argued, contrary to centuries of political teaching, that an energetic national government was compatible with, indeed essential to,

popular government. The national government described in *The Federalist* would have, for its "first object," the protection of the "diversity in the faculties of men, from which the rights of property originate."

Property and diversity were essential parts of the Federalist solution to the problem of popular government. Republics throughout history, the Federalists knew, had been torn asunder by the bitter struggle of political factions formed around opposing ideologies or around extreme inequalities of wealth. The American republic would escape that fate; a citizenry interested, above all, in the acquisition of property or wealth would have little time for ideological disputation or patience with it. And a modern commercial nation, organized for the acquisition of property and thus characterized by the division of labor, would be fragmented into such a diversity or "multiplicity of interests" that the great, fatal struggle of rich and poor would be averted. But commerce requires large markets, and large markets require "a great extent of territory"—sufficiently great that an energetic national government is necessary for its administration. The problem of fatal republican division, *The Federalist* argued, would not arise in the large commercial republic, administered by an energetic national government.

The Federalists understood that there was a certain unloveliness about the commercial republic. It relied upon and encouraged the vigorous pursuit of wealth—not always a pleasant spectacle. But "multiplying the means of gratification" and "promoting the introduction and circulation of the precious metals, those darling objects of human avarice and enterprise," were the only ways to "vivify the channels of industry and . . . make them flow with greater activity and copiousness"; that is, they were the only ways to promote the "prosperity of commerce" that had become the "primary object" of "all enlightened statesmen." National prosperity would be assured only if there were adequate economic incentives for the self-interested individual; Hamilton's *Report on Manufactures* was a blueprint for the creation of such incentives.

The Founders also realized that the pursuit of wealth would result in inequalities among men, given the "different and unequal faculties of acquiring property." But, as Hamilton argued, inequality followed inevitably from the freedom that the large commercial republic made possible: "An inequality would exist as long as liberty existed.... It would inevitably result from that liberty itself." Inequality was a small price to pay for liberty, according to the Federalists.

This Federalist "package" of principles—an energetic national government administering a large territory, commerce, national diversity, individual self-interest, and inequality, all in the name of prosperity and liberty—forms one great tradition of American political thought. It is certainly the primary tradition, given the success of the Federalists in incorporating their principles into the Constitution. But it is by no means the only tradition of American political thought, as the late Herbert Storing reminded us. The Federalists were challenged at the time of the Founding by what came to be called Anti-Federalism. Professor Storing was the first to make clear that the Anti-Federalists were *for* something, and what they were for had a powerful appeal in 1787 and continued to have a powerful appeal throughout American history. The Founding did not settle everything, according to Storing (1981, p. 3):

It did not finish the task of making the American polity. The political life of the community continues to be a dialogue, in which the Anti-Federalist concerns and principles still play an important part.... [In fact] the Anti-Federalists are entitled ... to be counted among the Founding Fathers.

THE ANTI-FEDERALISTS

The Anti-Federalists shared with the Federalists a commitment to popular government and liberty. This fundamental
consensus made possible the Founding, and gave the ratification debates the air of a quarrel within the family rather
than of a civil war. But the Anti-Federalists dissented from
the view that popular government or republicanism was
possible in a vast extent of territory and under an energetic central government. The main reason for the Anti-
Federalists' dissent was their belief, taken from Montesquieu, that republicanism was possible only with public-
spirited or virtuous citizens. Republican citizens had to be
imbued with the "love of the laws of our country"; they had
to exhibit a "constant preference of public to private interest." Only an alert, public-spirited citizenry, they believed,
would give that amount of attention to public affairs that
self-government or republicanism truly required.

This kind of virtue arose only in a genuine community,
where citizens sensed their oneness with their fellows.
Community, however, exacted a price: human differences
could not be permitted to flourish to such an extent that certain citizens considered themselves, or were considered by
others, to be outside the community. Thus, the Anti-
Federalists argued for a homogeneous citizenry: "In a republic, the manners, sentiments, and interests of the people
should be similar. If this could not be the case, there will be a
constant clashing of opinions." They had in mind, as Storing
argues, a homogeneity of a certain kind, "a society in which
there are no extremes of wealth, influence, education, or
anything else—the homogeneity of a moderate, simple,
sturdy, and virtuous people." Diversity was to be suppressed
on behalf of a general equality, because the Anti-Federalists
saw, in the words of the "Federal Farmer," a connection be-

tween "the equal division of our lands" and the "strong and manly habits of our people."

It was not only necessary that wealth be roughly equally distributed, but also that there not be too much of it. Too much wealth tended to draw attention away from public things and to corrupt republican morality. Thus, frugality or austerity was important for the Anti-Federalists, who agreed with John Adams that "frugality is a great revenue, besides curing us of vanities, levities, and fopperies, which are real antidotes to all great, manly, and warlike virtues."

Finally—and we come to the specific point of dissent from the Federalists' large republic—all these rigorous conditions for community could be had only in a small republic. Here again, the Anti-Federalists claimed as their authority Montesquieu, who argued that "it is natural for a republic to have only a small territory," because in "an extensive republic, the public good is sacrificed to a thousand private views." In a small republic, the "interest of the public is more obvious, better understood, and more within the reach of every citizen"; thus, public affairs would command sustained public attention. That is the reason the Anti-Federalists championed a modified confederal form of government for the new nation, in which primary political responsibility was left to the "small republics" in the states.

To the Federalists' strong national government over an extensive territory, the Anti-Federalists preferred a weak national government, with primary political power left to the states. That was because the Anti-Federalists preferred a republic animated by civic virtue or public-spiritedness to one animated by commerce and individual self-interest; a republic resembling a homogeneous community to one characterized by diversity, or a multiplicity of interests; a republic that insured a general equality to one that tolerated the inequalities that spring from liberty; and a republic with an austere, frugal—what we would call "no-growth"—economy to one that encouraged prosperity, growth, and luxury.

It is impossible to survey the principles of Anti-Federalism without acknowledging their appeal or sensing the power of their dissent from the Federalist position. And it would be regrettable if we, as a nation, had to accept one "package" of principles to the utter exclusion of the other. Fortunately, Americans are not faced by that unhappy choice. For the Federalists, while writing into the Constitution most of their principles and thus giving us the large commercial republic, did not have it all their own way in 1787.

OUR COEXISTENT TRADITIONS

The Anti-Federalists pressed hard at the Constitutional Convention for mitigation of the nationalist scheme of government proposed originally by Madison, Randolph, and others. The result of their efforts was what we call today (confusingly, in light of its Anti-Federalist source) federalism — the constitutional principle that important governing powers would be left to the states, and that certain parts of the national government, especially the electoral college and the Senate, would acknowledge in their structure the states as states. As the late Martin Diamond argued so persuasively, American federalism sends a decentralizing impulse through the American system: "The formal federal elements . . . permanently commit American government to decentralization and generate the informal political processes and behavior which keep the commitment a reality." Our constitutional commitment to federalism insures that state and local governments survive, and that they continue to supply some of the goods valued by the Anti-Federalists. Largely as a result of Anti-Federalist efforts, we have a federalism that preserves and nourishes local community attachments, civic virtue, and public-spiritedness, as well as a large, commercial republic that secures prosperity and liberty.

No one understood better than Alexis de Tocqueville the complex coexistence of Federalist large republicanism and Anti-Federalist small republicanism in American life. According to Tocqueville, Americans had "forcibly reconciled" those "two theoretically irreconcilable systems." There was no name for the government that resulted; it was a kind of "incomplete national government," which combined "the various advantages of large and small size for nations."

America was so prosperous, Tocqueville understood, because it was a large, commercial republic; it had given "free scope to the unguided strength and common sense of individuals." There were dangers in the individualistic pursuit of wealth, however, since it is "always an effort" for commercial men "to tear themselves away from their private affairs and pay attention to those of the community; the natural inclination is to leave the only visible and permanent representative of collective interests, that is to say, the state, to look after them." That was, of course, the ideal condition for tyranny. Furthermore, commerce could be dehumanizing, since "love of comfort" introduces the individual to "petty aims, but the soul clings to them; it dwells on them every day.... In the end they shut out the rest of the world and sometimes come between the soul and God."

Countering these tendencies, Tocqueville argued, were the American traditions of local self-government and private association—traditions kept alive by the decentralizing impulse of federalism. American lawgivers had wisely given "each part of the land its own political life so that there would be an infinite number of occasions for the citizens to act together and so that every day they should feel they depended on one another." Private voluntary associations of all kinds similarly served to draw men upward from mere self-interest into public life, combating the dehumanizing effects of individualism. Citizens acting together and depending on one another come to form a genuine community; a certain public-spiritedness or civic virtue is generated by local self-government, and men come to love their "little republic." Such public-spirited citizens, Tocqueville noted, will not be likely to surrender control of public life to the state.

For Tocqueville, then, the "forceable reconciliation" of "two theoretically irreconcilable systems" was absolutely central to the survival of American liberty. When he inquired into the "main causes tending to maintain a democratic republic in the United States," the first cause was "the federal form . . . which allows the Union to enjoy the power of a great republic and the security of a small one." The two systems or principles would always be in tension, according to Tocqueville, each threatening to consume the other. For instance, in Tocqueville's time the states were powerful enough to challenge the existence of the union. The real danger, however, lay in the future, when a centralized national government would threaten to swallow up the local institutions so important for liberty.

The greatest political crisis of our history—the Civil War—was precipitated precisely by the need to restore the balance between the two principles. Abraham Lincoln had to remind Americans that the principle of local government could not be radicalized into "squatter sovereignty"—that there was a certain moral minimum (in this case, the equality espoused in the Declaration of Independence) to which we were committed as a nation. With this great exception, however, the tension between Federalism and Anti-Federalism was a healthy and invigorating one throughout our first century and a half, one counterbalancing and modifying the other. We prospered as a great commercial nation and, at the same time, civic virtue and public-spiritedness thrived in our state and local governments and private associations.

THE NEW DEAL SYNTHESIS

The central claim of modern liberalism—or at least of that strain that runs from Theodore Roosevelt's "New National-

ism" to Franklin D. Roosevelt's "New Deal"—is that it could
resolve the tension between these two principles, collapsing
them into one coherent doctrine and giving us the best of
each. That is, liberalism, through the energetic government
established by the Federalists, promised to create on a national scale the sense of community thought possible by the
Anti-Federalists only in the small republic.

Essential to the creation of the "Great Community" (John
Dewey's description of the liberal goal) is the reduction,
by a powerful central government, of those community-
disrupting inequalities that spring from modern industrialism. According to Theodore Roosevelt, "The people . . .
have but one instrument which they can efficiently use
against the colossal combinations of business—and that
instrument is the government of the United States." Modern
liberalism, in Herbert Croly's famous formulation, would
fulfill the "promise of American life" by marrying Jefferson-
ian democracy—characterized by the "good fellowship" that
comes from "life in a self-governing community"—to
Hamiltonian nationalism. This promise to combine into one
coherent whole what had theretofore been considered rival
political traditions would give the New Deal public philosophy an overwhelming moral and political appeal.

A comprehensive account of the liberal idea would have to
begin with the appearance of Croly's *The Promise of American Life* in 1909, where the marriage of principles was first
described, and continue through Theodore Roosevelt's presidential campaign of 1912, when this new brand of liberalism
was injected into American political life, to Franklin
Roosevelt's New Deal, the apotheosis of modern liberalism.
Here, however, we will consider primarily the mature form of
liberalism, the New Deal public philosophy.

The New Deal public philosophy, according to Samuel
Beer, had two characteristic elements: centralization and
egalitarianism. Centralization meant that the national
government—as opposed to the state governments that

traditionally had been central to Democratic party doctrine—would now do what needed to be done to meet the
crisis of the Great Depression. This was far more than a
doctrine of administrative centralization; in fact, FDR hoped
to create a true sense of national community—characterized
by public-spiritedness, discipline, and self-sacrifice—in the
face of national problems. In his first inaugural address,
Roosevelt urged us to "move as a trained and loyal army willing to sacrifice for the goal of a common discipline." We had
to be prepared to "submit our lives and property to such discipline," and to exhibit "a unity of duty hitherto evoked only
in time of armed strife."

Essential to the task of creating national unity, according
to FDR, was the amelioration of extreme inequalities of
wealth or power that make community difficult—as the
Anti-Federalists had noted a century and a half before.
Hence, the second theme of the New Deal: egalitarianism.
Some of FDR's programs, such as the social security system,
involved a mild degree of wealth redistribution. Other
measures, such as the National Labor Relations Act of 1935,
served to reduce differences in power and influence between
the corporations and unions.

An energetic central government, fostering equality by
reducing disparities of wealth and power and cultivating in
the people a certain public-spirited devotion to the general
good, would, in Beer's words, further the "process of national
integration" in which "the community . . . is made more of a
community." That was the liberal promise: the creation of
the small republic within the large republic, the marriage of
Federalism and Anti-Federalism.

COMMUNITY VERSUS COMMERCE

It would be more accurate, of course, to describe the promise
of liberalism as the marriage of the *best* in Federalism with

the *best* in Anti-Federalism. Like all proposed marriages of
principles in which only the best elements of each are retained and the worst of each dropped, this proposed marriage
was utopian.

Modern liberalism promised community—but now *without*
the state, local, and private institutions that the Anti-
Federalists had considered the very source of community.
Liberals were, in fact, hostile to local institutions, as such
institutions were notoriously backward and provincial. As
Arthur Schlesinger, Jr., put it recently, "Local government
historically has been the . . . last refuge of reaction." It was
no longer necessary to pay the price of provincialism for
community, however; liberalism's "Great Community" would
be drawn together by a powerful, progressive national
government, and especially by a powerful, progressive president, using his office as a "bully pulpit" to preach selfless
devotion to the common national good.

Liberalism also promised to sustain the material abundance of the commercial republic—but this time *without* the
unattractive self-interested individualism and inequality
that the Federalists had considered the source of abundance.
Those unsavory features of commerce would gradually be
supplanted by community and public-spiritedness, apparently without harming commerce itself. In short, liberals
promised prosperity, while harboring suppressed hostilities
toward the traditional sources of prosperity. Liberals
assumed that abundance was here to stay and that we could
now get on with the task of assuring a more equitable distribution of abundance in the name of community.

Theodore Roosevelt therefore was able to argue that "the
most pressing problems that confront the present century
are not concerned with the material production of wealth,
but with its distribution." The business world could now
"change from a competitive to a co-operative basis," tran-
scending the pure free enterprise system, in which citizens
are "trodden down in the ferocious scrambling rush of unreg-

ulated and purely individualistic industrialism." FDR similarly believed the depression had shown that "heedless self-interest" was "bad economics" as well as "bad morals," and that "the greatest change we have witnessed has been the change in the moral climate in America." Roosevelt rejoiced that "our country has been knit together in a closer fellowship of mutual interest and common purpose," that "more and more of our people ... seek the greater good of the greater number," and that the "selfish purpose of personal gain, at our neighbor's loss, less strongly asserts itself."

The utopianism implicit in the prospect of a great national community, which would combine sustained prosperity with widespread and increasing equality, became apparent in the 1960s and 1970s. In particular, equality became the consuming passion of liberalism and, embodied in a growing central government, began to cut deeply into liberty and prosperity. Liberalism less and less successfully suppressed its hostility toward the necessary preconditions of growth. Anti-Federalist community began to devour Federalist commerce.

The growing liberal devotion to equality manifested itself primarily, of course, in a concern over the proper distribution of wealth. That concern had begun modestly enough as the desire to provide a floor for the least fortunate, and thereby bring them into the national community. The desire to provide a floor, however, swelled into a passion to eliminate all distinctions in the distribution of wealth—the assumption being that property was not private, but at the disposal of the community. Christopher Jencks would argue that "we need to establish the idea that the Federal government is responsible not only for the total amount of the national income, but for its distribution," and that we would have to "alter people's basic assumptions about the extent to which they are responsible for their neighbors and their neighbors for them." The assumption in John Rawls's *A Theory of Justice* was that everything—including an individual's talents and abilities—belonged to the community. The notion that the community was now responsible for the proper distribution of wealth was reflected in the proliferation of federal social welfare programs in the 1960s and 1970s and in the national tax structure, which came to be seen as a device for income transfer as much as for collection of revenues.

As the community demanded a more equitable distribution of wealth, it also demanded tighter government supervision of the economy in general. In the "ferocious scrambling rush" of commerce, the public good all too often was sacrificed to a variety of private goods. The national government had to remedy this imbalance—and so, throughout the 1960s and 1970s, it became deeply involved in the regulation of commerce on behalf of "community values" like public safety and clean air and water. All these redistributive and regulatory projects, of course, meant bigger and bigger government. The second principle of the New Deal—centralization—assumed proportions unanticipated by liberalism's founders.

The single-minded pursuit of community and equality through heavy taxes, massive regulation, and social engineering recently began to take a toll on national economic performance. It became increasingly apparent that Anti-Federalist community and equality and Federalist commercial prosperity were *not* so easily reconciled. This, of course, was something that the Anti-Federalists had seen long ago, when they had argued that a simple economy, frugality, and austerity were the only routes to community. It is not surprising, then, that this Anti-Federalist idea found an echo in liberal pronouncements as the economy slowed down in the late 1970s. Liberals no longer even tried to suppress their hostility toward the preconditions of commerce. The very principles of prosperity and growth were questioned, and the virtues of austerity, frugality, and a no-growth economy endorsed. Even President Carter would say in his inaugural address that "we have learned that *more* is not necessarily *better.*"

The problem would have been seen clearly by Tocqueville. In his eyes, the American experiment was successful because we had kept the two great American traditions apart, each in its appropriate sphere, yet in a healthy tension. The effort to marry the principles, however, had joined centralization (now free of its vital counterweight of local government) to equality (now lacking its vital counterweight of individual liberty). Relieved of their ballasts, equality and centralization had moved toward their logical conclusions and become radicalized. The result was a doctrine that drove us toward "a great nation in which every citizen resembles one set type and is controlled by one single power."

RESTORING THE "ESSENTIAL TENSION"

If, in fact, the New Deal public philosophy is dead or dying, it is because the utopian character of the marriage of Federalism and Anti-Federalism has become clear, on a practical level, to the American people. They simply are not prepared to pay the price of a redistributive tax structure, massive welfare programs, a powerful and intrusive central government, and a no-growth economy in order to achieve the liberal vision of the great national community.

Any public philosophy that would replace the New Deal, however, must return for its elements to the two American political traditions, for they both express immutable yearnings in the American soul. Neither tradition may be ignored. Contemporary conservatism (or, at any rate, libertarianism) and contemporary radical liberalism fail to understand this. Each of these strains of political thought does avoid the utopian excess of collapsing together the two political traditions. Each, however, commits the equally utopian excess of radicalizing one tradition at the expense of the other. Thus libertarianism (and its nineteenth-century precursor, laissez-faire capitalism) makes the error of radicalizing the liberty, self-interest, and commerce of the Federalist tradition while ignoring the equally legitimate impulse toward community and public-spiritedness. Conversely, the contemporary Left embraces only the Anti-Federalist principles of community and equality—and, in some of its more exotic manifestations, even the Anti-Federalist "small sphere"—while despising the principles of self-interest and commerce.

America will be returned to political health only if we avoid these utopian errors and restore the Tocquevillian condition in America. Both traditions must be resurrected and restored to their appropriate spheres. They will then function as they functioned prior to the New Deal: together, yet in tension, one correcting and moderating the excesses that follow from the other.

The new terms of political discourse in Washington suggest an awareness of this need to restore the Tocquevillian condition. We seem to have rediscovered the Federalist idea that one of government's primary concerns is the provision of incentives for individual economic enterprise. Restoring the "prosperity of commerce" through the stimulation of individual self-interest has once again become the "primary object" of our statesmen, at least momentarily. Nor does this concern with reviving the economy signify an abandonment of the principle of community. Rather, we now look again— with the Anti-Federalists and Tocqueville—to state and local government and private associations to satisfy the American yearning for community. The new terms of political discourse indicate a sort of instinctive return to the healthy separateness and tension of the two American political traditions.

Whether these new terms of political discourse become the *permanent* terms remains to be seen. The supreme test will be whether a comprehensive, politically persuasive alternative to the utopian vision of the New Deal can be formed from the two American political traditions. To that end, this administration must make explicit what is already implicit in its programs of supply-side economics on the one hand, and the "New Federalism" and private sector initiatives on the other.

This is by no means assured, of course, for the utopian vision of the great national community continues to have tremendous appeal in America. From the vantage of modern liberalism, supply-side economics appears to be simply a return to unrestrained individualism and mean-spirited self-aggrandizement. This economic program, by "taking from the poor and giving to the rich," can only compound the inequalities that liberalism has painstakingly ameliorated over the past five decades. Supply-side economics is, in short, a profound repudiation of the principle of community. The same may be said of the new concern with local and private institutions. Local and private communities are anachronistic, parochial "refuges of reaction"—mere mockeries of the great, progressive national community that, in liberalism's view, is the proper goal for America. In its struggle for survival, modern liberalism promises to take full advantage of the moral high ground that comes with the defense of the principle of community.

Contemporary American politics will be characterized for some time to come by the struggle between an as yet vaguely formulated Tocquevillian view of America, and a well formulated but politically exhausted liberal utopian view. However this contest is decided, it cannot be understood until we first understand its theoretical components—the two great traditions of American political thought.

3

DANIEL J. ELAZAR

American Federalism Today: Practice versus Principle

New thinking about federalism. Organizational pyramids. Contractual noncentralization. The federal matrix. Managerialism and the pyramid. Revitalizing federal democracy.

Now in its second year, the Reagan administration is turning its attention to the state of the federal system in order to fulfill the president's promise to strengthen the states within that system and thereby strengthen the system as a whole. In principle, this should be an easy task—simply have the

federal government return or turn over certain functions to
the states, free revenue sources to accompany them, and
reduce federal regulatory interventions into state affairs and
the process of state governance.

Unfortunately, that is far easier said than done, as suc-
cessive administrations since the Nixon presidency have discovered. There are several reasons why this is so:

- Even when there is general agreement in principle,
  there is great disagreement around the country and
  even within the administration as to what shall be
  turned over to the states. This administration is no more
  immune to this problem than any other; indeed, its
  people have suggested new federal interventions almost
  as frequently as withdrawals.

- The states are not necessarily willing to accept added
  responsibilities. As we have seen at recent governors' con-
  ferences, they often have to be forced to be free.

- There is a reliance on simple notions of separating federal
  and state functions as a basis for policymaking rather
  than on strengthening the states by restoring classic patterns of intergovernmental cooperation. Much of this
  problem relates to a misunderstanding of the principles of
  federalism and how they informed the American political
  system in better days.

Whatever the problematics of the practice of American
federalism today, there is, indeed, a crisis in American thinking about federalism. To see that this is so, one need only
look at most of the literature on the subject published during
the past two decades explaining, justifying, or advocating
particular courses of governmental action in the name of
federalism. It is time for an infusion of new thinking about
the federal principle and its practical implications on the
American scene.

A call for new thinking does not imply that there has been
no thinking, only that what has become the conventional

thinking over the past generation is overwhelmingly deriv-
ative and increasingly confused. Nor does it imply that old
ideas are necessarily outmoded, only that even the best
ideas—those of eternal worth—need to be periodically
reanalyzed and reformulated.

Let us begin from the beginning. American culture is
strongly (though not exclusively) oriented toward commerce,
particularly in questions of organizational efficiency. This
has had important intellectual consequences, one of which
has been that American ideas about governmental organizational efficiency tend to be derived from the world of commerce, particularly in its business manifestations. But there
is normally a lag of a generation or so from the time new
ideas emerge in the business world and the time they are applied to government.

The thrust of American government from the beginning of
the twentieth century has been toward greater centralization within a hierarchical model. This is in no small part
the result of reformers' efforts, conscious or unconscious, to
transfer to government the mode of organization adopted by
big business a generation earlier. The great entrepreneurs
who built their enterprises after the Civil War and Reconstruction maintained tight personal control at the top.
Transferred to the government realm, their model led to
emphasis on a very powerful president responsible for setting policy and administering it through an elaborate
bureaucratic structure responsible to him. Congress was
judged by how rapidly it provided the legislation and funds
that the president requested. Present dissatisfactions with
this model have their sources in the widespread feeling that
presidential power has run away with itself in both foreign
and domestic spheres, while the administrative pyramid has
become too large to be controlled from the top yet too broad
to be controlled at any other point.

By the time American reformers and politicians were leading the country into centralized hierarchical arrangements,

business planners were beginning to question the efficacy of
tight pyramids in organizing complex enterprises. Their
answer was to keep the pyramid but to loosen it; namely,
decentralization. After World War II government rolled on
toward more hierarchy while business moved to implement
the decentralization model. In the late 1960s—a generation
later—that model entered the governmental arena in the
form of Richard Nixon's "New Federalism," which was
designed to be an answer to the problem of overcentralization or too much hierarchy.

In the New Federalism, the pyramid model was retained
and strengthened, but the emphasis was on decentralizing
operations within it. From regional arrangements within the
federal government to the delegation to the states and localities of authority to enforce federal standards, it represented
a new thrust toward decentralization. Unfortunately, all
good intentions notwithstanding, the overall result was a
series of administrative efforts that increased federal dom-
inance over the states and localities in crucial policy and program areas (ostensibly balanced by the decentralization of
administrative powers over those areas), and an effort to expand radically the powers of the president over the funding
of all federal and cooperative programs. The ambivalent approach of the Nixon administration was continued in a bipartisan way in the Ford and Carter years.

THE FEDERALIST MODEL

But pyramids, tight or loose, are not the real way of American government. From the very first, the American system
was organized as a matrix, not a hierarchy—a noncentralized political system in which the powers were not allocated
by "levels" but divided among different arenas—federal,
state, and local. The original model of American federalism

was closely related to the market model of many small enterprises of approximately equal size functioning within a relatively restricted framework, which was the model of American commerce before the industrial revolution that influenced the original shape of American government under the Constitution.

In strictly governmental terms, federalism is a form of political organization that unites separate polities within an overarching political system so that all maintain their fundamental political integrity. It distributes power among general and constituent governments so that they all share in the system's decision-making and executing processes. In a larger sense, federalism represents the linking of free people and their communities through lasting but limited political arrangements to protect certain rights and achieve specific common ends while preserving the respective integrities of participants.

Federal democracy is an authentic American contribution to democratic thought and republican government. It represents a synthesis of the Puritan idea of the covenant relationship as the foundation of all proper human society and the constitutional ideas of English "natural rights" schools of the seventeenth and early eighteenth centuries. The covenant idea (*foedus,* the Latin root of the word "federal," means covenant or compact), which the Puritans took from the Bible, demands a different kind of political relationship (and perhaps, in the long run, a different kind of human relationship) than theories of mass democracy that have attracted many adherents since the French Revolution. It emphasizes partnership between individuals, groups, and governments in the pursuit of justice; cooperative relationships that make the partnership real; and negotiation among the partners as the basis for sharing power. The Lockean understanding of the social compact as the basis for civil society represents a secularized version of the covenant principle. The synthesis of the two forms undergirds the original American political vision.

Contractual noncentralization—the structured dispersion of power among many centers whose legitimate authority is constitutionally guaranteed—is the key to the widespread and entrenched diffusion of power that remains the principle characteristic of federal democracy. Noncentralization is not the same as decentralization, though the latter term is frequently—and erroneously—used in its place to describe the American system. Decentralization implies the existence of a central authority, a central government. The government that can *de*centralize can *re*centralize if it so desires. Hence, in decentralized systems the diffusion of power is actually a matter of grace, not right, and as history reveals, in the long run it is usually treated as such.

In a noncentralized political system, power is so diffused that it cannot legitimately be centralized or concentrated without breaking the structure and spirit of the constitution. The United States has such a noncentralized system. We have a national—or general—government that functions powerfully in many areas for many purposes, but it is not a central government controlling all the lines of political communication and decision making. Our states are not creatures of the federal government but, like the latter, derive their authority directly from the people. Structurally, they are substantially immune from federal interference. Functionally, they share many activities with the federal government but without necessarily forfeiting their policy-making roles and decision-making powers. In short, they are polities, not administrative subdivisions.

In contemporary social science terminology, centralization and decentralization are extremes of the same continuum while noncentralization represents another continuum altogether. In systems of the former type, it is rather simple to measure the flow of power one way or another. In noncentralized systems, however, such measurement is considerably more difficult. In the American case, for example, simple evidence of national government involvement in a particular field does not tell us enough about the relative strength of the various power centers in policy-making, administration, or what-have-you. The primary diffusion of power makes "involvement" take on many different meanings. As those involved in the governmental process well know, even apparently unilateral programs may be substantially shaped by the other governments through the political process. As those working in local government also know, he who pays the piper may or may not call the tune, and not necessarily in proportion to the amount of money provided.

To return to the image with which we began, decentralization implies hierarchy, a pyramid of governments with gradations of power flowing down from the top. This image is used almost as a matter of course by figures serving on all planes of government, without any thought to its larger implications. But it is misleading and distorts reality. It took the development of the most recent technology, that of the space frontier, to open the eyes of some of us to the limits of a hierarchical approach to government. The technology of the space frontier—of the world of cybernetics—is based on the principle that efficiency comes from two sources: a good communications network and a certain amount of redundancy. Redundancy in literary English is usually interpreted to mean useless overlapping, or what American administrative reformers like to refer to as "duplication," a word no longer neutral in the American governmental lexicon. To the cyberneticists, however, redundancy is a means of providing "fail-safe" mechanisms to keep things working, on the assumption that errors will occur in any system and that the continued operation of the system—whether it be a machine or an organization—requires that there be other channels for the communications to pass through and other forces or factors able to initiate and respond to different actions.

The theory and experience of the new technology, in a word, stand in direct contradiction to earlier notions of duplication. Put differently, technology has begun to imitate the Constitution of the United States by following principles that our founders applied to government in the eighteenth century. The founders of our federal republic, taking due cognizance of what they understood to be a "new science of politics," created a political system based upon the very principles that now animate the new technology. That system was not some pyramid, with channels for giving orders from the top to the bottom, but a matrix of authoritative governmental units located within a framework provided by the Constitution. This matrix combined a national or general government—which could make authoritative decisions, especially on so-called "boundary" questions—with state governments equally authoritative within their areas of constitutional competence. The whole system was based upon the federal principle of redundancy, of more than one authoritative body responsible for the conduct of the government and capable of exercising its responsibilities.

The matrix of American government is written into the Constitution and is reflected in the territorial organization of American party politics. It is so much a part of American political culture that Washington, D.C., was consciously laid out in its image, with the executive, legislative, and judicial branches of government at different points in the matrix and the administrative offices originally placed between the first two (Young 1956). Despite efforts to replace this distribution of powers, the matrix survives as the fundamental reality of American government, albeit in an increasingly battered (and embattled) way.

Several things need to be noted about the American federal matrix. While it is composed of multiple centers, these centers are not separated unto themselves. They are bound together within a network of distributed powers with lines of communication and decision making that force them to interact. It is not the need for interaction or common action that is special here, but the form and character of that interaction—sharing through bargaining, or negotiated cooperation rather than directive.

The noncentralized communications network itself has two rigidly rooted anchors, as it must if the matrix is to exist. The general government (that nineteenth-century term has great merit for the precision and clarity it brings to the subject) sets the framework for the matrix as a whole by defining and delineating the largest arena. The states, whose boundaries are constitutionally fixed, provide the basic decision-making areas within the matrix. Both together provide the constitutional basis for the diffusion of powers necessary to prevent hierarchical domination, given the human penchant for hierarchies (see Diamond 1969).

THE FEDERALIST MODEL APPLIED . . .

The nation and each of the fifty states is a polity in its own right, in the fullest sense. While either the federal or state government may serve the others in some administrative capacity by mutual agreement, neither is designed to be the administrative arm of the others *per se* (see Elazar 1981). Nevertheless, since the beginning of the republic, the elements in the matrix have worked together to develop common policies and programs, with most important actors involved in important details of most steps in problem definition, planning, programming, budgeting, implementation, and evaluation of policies of mutual interest to them through the political process (Elazar 1966). That is the very heart of the argument of the cooperative federalists.

Students of federalism pointed this out empirically two decades ago and more through detailed case studies of federalism, the party political process, and the role of Congress, particularly in the quadrangle linking state (and/or local) administrators, their federal counterparts, congres-

sional representatives, and common professional associations or interest groups. Congressional/administrative preclearance of proposed legislation and administrative regulations is a regular feature of American government and
has been since 1790. Plans for programs are developed, more
often than not, in consultation with spokesmen for the interested parties. Unfortunately, the inroads of the new hier-
archs into the *manner* in which all this is done have become
increasingly great, to the point where the traditional system
is in serious jeopardy.

The problem, then, is not that the federal and state
governments must cooperate, but that the federal government, under the guise of "cooperative federalism," has
changed its role from being supportive—from playing a
"backstopping" role—to being coercive and even preemptive. That is what must be changed. The present administration is right to seek radical measures, since only by getting to
the root of the problem can the dangerous trends of the past
generation be reversed. But its strategy must begin by recognizing the interlocking character of the federal system, and
then it must seek a correct role for the federal government
within that system.

... AND PERVERTED

When, two generations ago, much needed to be accomplished
for the nation as a whole and only the federal government
seemed to have sufficient size and resources to assure that
what was instituted was done more or less equitably for citizens in all parts of the land, it was easy for the pyramid
model to win wide acceptance and for governors and
governed alike to operate according to it. In due time,
however, the pyramid approach was carried to its logical conclusion. The president of the United States somehow was

placed at its acme and the Congress at a level below him. Stated boldly, the federal government should deal with:

- application of the framing principles of the U.S. Constitution;

- extraterritorial issues (e.g., foreign affairs, defense);

- boundary questions among the constituent entities of the federal system;

- support of the states and their localities in matters of national concern.

It need not—indeed, should not—deal with any of these on an exclusive or preemptive basis. Nor should every branch of the federal government necessarily be involved in every one of these four fields. In most cases, except in aspects of the second, the federal role should be seemingly (in the sense of support of other governments or of the private sector) entered into reluctantly or because of special circumstances.

(In this, the academic community shares responsibility. Prominent spokesmen from universities argued forcibly that federal wishes and demands must inevitably take precedence over those of the states and localities as if the federal government were on top, and that presidential programs must be accepted uncritically by Congress as if presidents were inevitably right.) Finally, presidents began to believe their press notices. The results were the debacles of the 1960s and 1970s when one president brought us into an undeclared war that became one of the costliest in our history and led to public revulsion manifested even in the nation's streets, and another president brought us to Watergate.

The notion of the American system as pyramidal was reenforced by a convergence of Jacobin views of the polity and managerialist views of its administration, both of which gained currency in the United States in the late nineteenth century and became dominant in the twentieth.

The Jacobin model polity has power concentrated in a

single center that is more or less influenced by its periphery. Centralization is the organizational expression of Jacobinism, which distrusts dispersed power because of the European historical experience out of which it grew and in which localism was synonymous with support for the pre-revolutionary powerholders. V. I. Lenin and Harold Laski were perhaps the most articulate twentieth-century proponents of Jacobinism, Lenin in its totalitarian collectivist manifestation and Laski in its social democratic form.

Jacobinism was brought to the United States in the mid-nineteenth century as a form of liberalism. Francis Lieber, a German refugee and the first professional political scientist in America (he held a chair at Columbia University), was the first articulate proponent of Jacobin liberalism on the American scene. Beginning as a theoretical critique of the compact theory of the state (i.e., an attack on the theoretical basis of federalism), in the course of a generation it became linked with the new nationalism of the late nineteenth century in the development of a practical program of expanded national government activity. Woodrow Wilson then gave it a more Americanized form by suggesting that Congress was the natural center of all political power.

Managerialism was an organizational response to the industrial revolution, in many respects typically American but with strong roots in the military and bureaucratic traditions of Prussia and France. Politically, managerialism represents an effort to democratize (or, perhaps more accurately, republicanize) autocracy, whether in the immediate sense of the autocracy of the great entrepreneurs who built and ruled the great new industrial corporations, or in the older sense of imperial autocracy. In both cases, the Founders can be considered "conquerors" who ruled autocratically and, in the end, unsatisfactorily, given changing times. The introduction of managerial structures was designed to transform autocratic rule without formally altering the hierarchical institutional structures built by the Founders. The proponents of

Figure 1
The Jacobin Model

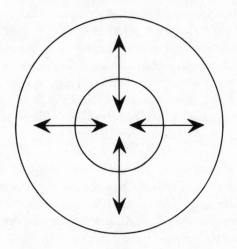

Figure 2
The Managerial Pyramid

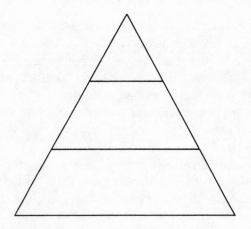

managerial techniques could argue that what they proposed was politically neutral and hence not a threat to the existing system. In fact, as new generations of managers emerged and as management became a career in its own right, managerialism became an ideology in its own right.

The pyramid structure is a key feature of managerialism. It goes without saying that the top must be the most important level and the place where decisions are made as to which level does what. Since proponents of managerialism never called it that and, indeed, believed that they were advocating a politically neutral means of increasing efficiency, the implications of its spread in the United States are just now beginning to be recognized. In fact, managerialism, for all its practical orientation and sincere commitment to neutrality in such matters, does reflect a political position that is no less real for not being articulated as such. In a scientific age committed to the relativity of ends, it was transformed by some from a mere technique into a potential vehicle for secular salvation that offered a right process in place of a teleology.

TWENTIETH-CENTURY SYNTHESES

As a practical matter, these three approaches have had to be related to one another in the conduct of American government during the twentieth century. What resulted were two separate syntheses fundamentally in conflict with one another. That conflict remained submerged as long as it did not affect the pursuit of immediate common goals. Today it is emerging as the old goals must be replaced by new ones intimately related to one approach or another.

In ideas, the synthesis was between Jacobinism and managerialism, both of which were useful to justify the increase in the size of government and its centralization during the past two generations. The synthesis itself grew out of (1) the managerial dimension of Progressivism, which saw in the new techniques of management a means to make government more efficient and economical; (2) Jacobin influences on liberal intellectuals, generally in Marxist form, which led them not only to advocate strong centralized government but to reconceptualize social and political life in terms of the center-periphery model; and (3) the practical experiences of the interwar generation which, when confronted by two total wars and an unprecedented depression, increasingly turned to government for direction and control and, at the same time, became at least somewhat disillusioned with inherited political ideas in the versions handed down to them (which they did not know differed from the original).

In practice, on the other hand, the synthesis was between managerialism and federalism, reflecting both the realities of American politics and the continuation of fondly supported traditional principles. That synthesis grew out of (1) the impetus of Progressivism toward restoring America's sense of community that was so threatened in an industrial age, as well as toward improving the efficiency of its governmental system; (2) the practical experiences of the interwar generation, which showed the need to introduce management techniques and bureaucratic organization into most governmental institutions yet did not lead to any fundamental changes in the federal system, even where articulate groups were willing to promote them; and (3) institutional and political constraints requiring managerial devices and ideas to adapt to a multicentered federal system—with politics remaining noncentralized and functioning through the separation of powers and a continued reliance on checks and balances.

THE OLD SYNTHESIS UNRAVELS

At first, the potential conflict between the two syntheses was avoided because activists were pursuing common goals; only

toward the end of the postwar generation did it become ir-
repressible. The emergence of that conflict can be traced
through three stages.

During stage one (1946–1964), the practical convergence
of the previous generation was maintained and even extended as the federal government reorganized to accommodate congressional and local interests. Increased intergovernmental cooperation and state governmental reorganiza-
tion on the federal model were the order of the day. At this
time, appropriate theories of management, bureaucracy, and
intergovernmental relations were developed to account for,
explain, and justify the new order of things.

Stage two (1964–1970) brought with it a new spirit of
federal activity based on a further extension of Jacobin ideas
supported by managerial goals. Whether intentional or not,
the "Great Society" programs represented the fulfillment of
the Jacobin-managerial synthesis through which Jacobin
goals were pursued through the intensive utilization of
managerial approaches and techniques. This stage saw a
redefinition of equality, democracy, and other American
values to fit Jacobin prescriptions, coupled with a redefinition of individualism that went beyond the ken of any of the
three approaches. In both its successes and failures, the
Great Society made thoughtful Americans begin to recognize
the limits of both politics and bureaucracy and, in the process, to question the two approaches as sources of secular
salvation.

After 1970, for the remaining six years of postwar generation and into the new generation now upon us, a third stage
can be distinguished in which the terms of the conflict are
slowly but surely being defined. The disillusionment with politics as a vehicle for solving deeply rooted social problems,
the bureaucracy problem, and the application of managerial
techniques for constitutionally questionable purposes in the
Nixon years were joined with a new questioning of the
assumptions of the Jacobin-managerial synthesis in some

academic circles. Certain names come immediately to mind. The late Martin Diamond brought us back to the original federalist sources of the American polity, thereby seriously questioning the authenticity and validity of prevalent Jacobin concepts of American institutions. Vincent and Elinor Ostrom synthesized the principles derived from those sources with those of public choice theory and used the results to measure the validity of current governmental policies and behavior, concluding that federalist theory was intrinsically correct as administrative as well as political doctrine and questioning the basic assumptions of managerialism. Martin Landau has rediscovered the virtues of redundancy, Heinz Eulau, the link between federalism and representation, and Samuel Beer, the virtues of the states, while Aaron Wildavsky has mercilessly exposed the fallacies of expecting special wisdom from the federal government. The journal *Publius* has become the forum for the expression and development of many of these ideas. Nevertheless, this reexamination is still in its early stages.

DECENTRALIZING THE FEDERAL SYSTEM

The suggestion that the American system is not pyramidal does not mean that there are no lines of authority within it. Some place, some time, decisions have to be made. If every "buck" need not stop at the president's desk, all must stop somewhere. That is why the matrix cannot be purely horizontal. There must be centers of power within it if there is not to be a single center of power. The choice is not between one center and none, but between one and many, with different ones taking precedence in different situations. The question, then, is which of the many centers are to be involved in which decisions, and how?

While under normal circumstances the elements in the

matrix work together to develop common policies and programs, the secret of preserving nonhierarchical relationships within the network lies precisely in the right of the elements not to act under certain conditions. Without that right, the search for consensus becomes an unending round of coercion on the part of one party or another. A distinction must be made between governmental activities that require the participation of all and those that do not, or that do not require joint participation. The Constitution was an attempt to deal with just this problem. In my opinion, it still provides a good basis for dealing with it. But the Framers never claimed that they had provided the ultimate answers for all time, or even all the answers for their time. By the very nature of things, it is a problem that recurs daily, especially in such a complex political and social system as ours.

There is no formula that can be developed once and for all to be applied automatically to each case. Instead, there must be a consensus that within constitutional limits the constituent units, as polities, can do what they will unless a strong case is made to the contrary. For some issue areas, that case is made *a priori* under the Constitution; for others, it is very murky indeed. Here, as in all other relationships within the federal system, it is not—and never has been—a "win-lose" proposition except in the minds of those who have dominated public discussion of the subject. If, as I am prepared to argue, the system itself is far less hierarchical today than their images of it, even after two generations of centralization, it is because of the system's own tough resilience and the rough-and-ready responses of the very untheoretical practitioners who make it work.*

---

*Since the days of Woodrow Wilson, the intellectual leaders in the field of public administration have been in the forefront of the hierarchy school. Now a new school of antihierarchs is emerging to provide intellectual leadership needed to topple the pyramids that have come to dominate American political thinking, if not American political life. Vincent Ostrom, Harlan Cleveland, Frederick Thayer, and others are taking the lead in a very important enterprise that, incidentally, is revitalizing the study of public administration. This literature is cited and described by Thayer in an unpublished paper prepared for the conference of the American Society for Public Administration in Los Angeles, April 1973. Vincent Ostrom (1974) has dealt with this question at length.

Because powers are really diffused—usually in a rather untidy way—throughout the matrix, it is very difficult to transfer power from Washington. Other presidents have discovered that in order to decentralize they must first centralize. Morton Grodzins pointed this out in 1959 in commenting on the failure of President Eisenhower's Joint Federal-State Action Committee to decentralize anything (Grodzins 1966). At that time the president lacked sufficient initial power to centralize, so he could not decentralize. Today, in an age of hierarchy-assumers, a president can successfully centralize but, as Grodzins then pointed out, there is no guarantee that an administration strong enough to overcome the noncentralization inherent in the system will willingly part with hard-won powers. Certainly the Nixon administration did not. At most, it was willing to pass on the hard choices to the states and localities, reserving to itself the basic powers in areas where there was potential positive payoff. For those of us who believe in the virtues of federalism, the substitution of decentralization for noncentralization is hardly an advance, no matter how untidy the latter may be.

FEDERALISM AND THE CURSES OF BIGNESS

Today Americans are confronted with the obvious failure of hierarchical structures that are not only unable to "deliver the goods," but have even come to distort the delivery system in pursuit of their own vested interests. We have discovered that, in very large bureaucracies, coordination is well-nigh impossible "at the top," since the people on the top can barely control their own organizations and are frequently at their mercy. Moreover, in a system of interlocking arenas (which is what exists in the United States despite all the talk about "levels"), there is no real "top" to do the coordinating.

Similarly, Americans have begun to note the failure of managerial techniques widely touted as means to come to grips with contemporary governmental problems. Certainly, the idea that they would automatically result in efficiency and economy has long since gone by the boards. We now know how bureaucracies create their own inefficiencies and diseconomies. Beyond that, there has been a discovery that the new management techniques (the Planning-Programming-Budgeting system and zero-based budgeting are prime examples) are inappropriate to the political arena with its lack of precise, agreed-upon goals, and its basic purposes of conciliating the irreconcilable and managing conflict.

On a different but closely related plane, Americans are beginning to sense the failure of "consumerism"—the redefinition of people primarily as consumers and their institutions primarily as vehicles for the satisfaction of consumer wants. At the very least, the redefinition of government as a service delivery mechanism and citizens as consumers leads to an unmanageable acceleration of public demands. It also leads to the evaluation of all institutions by a set of standards that, being human institutions, they are bound to fail. Not the least of its problems is the abandonment of the principle that people have responsibilities as well as rights, obligations to each other if not to the polity in the abstract, which, when neglected, imperil democracy by undermining its very foundations.

The problem remains: how can we restore the spirit and revitalize the practice of federal democracy? This means, in short, preserving noncentralization, freedom of choice, pluralism, and regional and group differences; maximizing liberty in tandem with equality; and assuring proper access and representation for citizens.

Three general principles could serve as the basis for any program of federal government decentralization undertaken at this time. They are:

• The revival of the notion of citizenship, or the reestablish-

ment of the principle that people are not simply consumers of government services but citizens of a polity—
indeed, multiple polities—with obligations as well as
rights.

- The revival of constitutionalism, or the reestablishment of
the principle that the federal government has limited
powers and cannot do everything it may wish.

- The revival of true partnership (intergovernmental and
interpersonal) with the reestablishment of the principle that more is gained by cooperation than through
compulsion.

All reorganizational proposals should be measured as to
whether or not they are in harmony with these principles,
which represent the foundations of a federalist standard
reflective of American values. Applying such principles, the
federal government properly becomes a framing institution
rather than a "central office" or the top of the pyramid. That
role is certainly vital and no diminution of the importance of
the federal government, but it is consistent with the intentions of the Founders.

On one level, these principles are relatively easily understood. On another, they are the subjects of eternal probing—
for their meaning and for the ways to apply them on a day-
to-day basis. Both of these tasks will continue to exist as long
as the United States does; should they cease, that in itself
would be a sign of the death of the American polity as we
know it.

Within the limits of a reality that will never conform as
closely to our models as we would like, and that might not
pass certain aesthetic tests, we need to strengthen the basic
noncentralization of the American system. We must reconceptualize our understanding of the federal system by
rediscovering the federal principle that underlies it—a principle that, in human terms, seeks to substitute coordinative
for hierarchical relationships to the maximum possible ex-

tent. I would like to believe that the Reagan administration offers Americans a great opportunity to revitalize federal democracy now.

4

STEPHEN L. SCHECHTER

The State of
American Federalism
in the 1980s

**Political and managerial concepts of federalism. The
grants-in-aid system. Accountability in government
functions. Turning back federal revenues. The reassessment process. Fiscal and constitutional issues.
The institutional challenge to the federal system.**

The first response of most people to crisis is pessimism. But
the really great nations of history have always been those that
turned moments of weakness into sources of strength, and
that came to see the crises they faced as opportunities for self-

improvement and self-correction. The American system has reached just such a pivotal moment. In the wake of the last decade of economic, social, and diplomatic upheaval, it is easy enough to take a pessimistic view of America's future. The very structure of our institutions—and especially of our governmental institutions—can be seen twisting and weakening under the strains of economic change. The recovery of prosperity and rapid growth has become not simply an economic but also a political imperative.

Those who have remained attentive to the original design of our governmental system—who have kept faith with federalism—can now point with dubious satisfaction to the role that a burgeoning federal government has played in the hobbling of our economy and the quiet demoralization of our citizens. If we seem unprepared psychologically and institutionally to come to terms with the task of recovery, then it is largely because our government and our citizens have lost touch with federalist principles. But that is precisely why the present crisis affords us an unprecedented opportunity to recover the federalist perspective as a way of recovering economic and political vitality. Moreover, it is essential that we do so, because only a federalist approach to our institutional problems will get at their root.

A NEW FEDERALISM FOR A NEW GENERATION?

In a truly healthy federal system, the challenge of economic recovery would be seen from the start as a challenge simultaneously facing all planes of government, because viable markets and meaningful powers could be found on all planes. But such a claim—that this is a truly nonhierarchical society in which the federal principles of self-rule and shared rule prevail—can no longer be made for the American system.

Over the past fifteen years the United States has crossed the fault line from a federal system to a decentralized national system; and, unhappily, the concept of "cooperative federalism" has been wrongly used to justify that crossing. The cynical explanation for this is that the states would not say "yes" to a host of costly social initiatives, and Congress could not say "no." But while there is always some truth in cynical interpretations, a more complete explanation would have to begin with the change in the very way Americans have come to conceptualize politics and the American system.

Whatever the reason, the operating model of American politics today leaves little room for federalism. When it comes time to make policy, all eyes look to Washington, and federalism is viewed as one among many cross-pressures rather than as a pathway through them. When it comes time to implement policy, federalism is transformed into a managerial model in which the states and localities are cast in the roles of middle and lower echelons of management that cannot be trusted to follow orders without being paid off and reined in. The political idea of states as polities and localities as communities has all but disappeared.

In 1981 the Reagan administration took a significant first step toward restoring federalism to its proper place in the theory and practice of American politics. But one gets a sense of how difficult this will yet be when, on 28 July 1981, liberal reconciliation conferees found it easier to support funds for "chastity centers" (originally proposed by Alabama Senator Jeremiah Denton) than for a family planning block grant for the states, and conservative conferees found it easier to trade off up to 44 percent of those funds for a pregnant teenagers' program, created at the urging of Eunice Kennedy Shriver, than to fight for the states.

The implication in all this is clear: before the country can embark on some kind of "New Federalism" it must first relearn what it means to be federalist. And this requires rediscovering the federalist principles of "self-rule, shared rule" and learning how to apply them to the challenges of today. It is to the description of this task that the remainder of this paper is devoted.

ATTEMPTS TO UNWIND THE SYSTEM

For a hundred and fifty years, from the Constitutional Convention of 1787 to the constitutional revolution of 1937, the operating premise of American intergovernmental relations centered on the commonsense notion that "good fences make good neighbors." There were indeed a variety of close "working relations" among all planes of government; and, paradoxically, those relations were strongest in the fields of education and transportation, which are now touted as traditionally local and state functions. But there also was a safe "political distance" in the working relations between the federal government and state and local governments. This distance was maintained by the consent theory of limited government and subsequently modernized in the doctrines of dual federalism and laissez-faire economics.

This is the lesson of history that has been eroded by the centralization of government since 1937. In all of the talk for and against "transferring authority back to the states" and "sorting out functions," we have forgotten that what we have really lost is the old-fashioned virtue of "reservedness" in thinking about government. The simple fact is that all planes of government are doing too many wrong things and in too imperious a manner, whether in their dealings with citizens or with each other. In the absence of standards setting the limits of governmental power, governments have become unreserved in their decisions about when to use power and how to share it. This, in my opinion, is the main cause for the sorry state of both American federalism and the American economy.

Hence, I submit that the leading challenge before us is intellectual and that this challenge can be assisted but not replaced by current institutional efforts to unwind the system. Let me illustrate this point by introducing what I consider to be federalist cautions to guide each of the efforts to unwind the system—enhancing the flexibility of states in the implementation of existing programs, sorting out governmental functions, turning back federal revenues to the states, and deregulating the federal system.

Enhancing Flexibility in the Grants-in-Aid System

In 1980 the 96th Congress took some steps toward enhancing the flexibility of state and local governments in the implementation of federal grants. One such effort was the Regulatory Flexibility Act, which requires federal agencies to assess the impact of their rules and paperwork requirements on small businesses and governments. Another such effort was renewal of the Joint Funding Simplification Act, which permits grantees to pool federal funds from different sources to be used for a common project.

However, these small steps toward flexibility in the administrative process pale by comparison to the lack of progress in enhancing flexibility in the selection process. This, of course, requires a measure of trust in state and local decision making that was decidedly absent from congressional deliberations. The most widely publicized instance of this was the heated congressional debate over the state share of revenue sharing, which culminated in the adoption of the interesting but somewhat demeaning Levitas amendment, requiring that the states return an equal amount of categorical grant funds in order to receive general revenue-sharing funds in fiscal year (FY) 1982 and FY 1983. Less publicized but no less vexing was the limitation placed on the use of home mortgage revenue bonds.

During the first year of the 97th Congress, Reagan administration proposals sought an across-the-board enhancement of flexibility in the grant process through the consolidation of eighty-eight categorical programs into seven block grants. In response, Congress combined fifty-seven categorical grants into nine block grants in the FY 1982 budget.

While many of the more substantial and controversial programs were carved out of the block grant proposals, some $10.2 billion remained. As reported in a recent issue of *National Journal* (Cohen 1981, p. 1416), the National Governors' Association (NGA) sees this as "a change in direction from restrictive to flexible federal aid—but not a dramatic shift." According to the NGA, the net effect will be to increase flexible federal aid to states and localities from 18 percent of total aid received in FY 1981, and only 16.5 percent in the proposed Carter budget, to 23 percent in the recently adopted congressional budget. Additionally, a restrictive House provision, which would have required states to prove programs to be ineffective before substantially diminishing support for them, was watered down to a less rigorous reporting requirement.

There is room for caution in this current block grant effort; and for this writer, it centers less on whether results to date are viewed as partial successes or partial failures than on whether there are long-term dangers in relying on the block grant approach. By comparison with the present state of restrictive categorical programs, the 1981 block grants substantially enhance state and local flexibility. But for how long? The history of the 1970s shows that block grants may be more susceptible to congressional and bureaucratic control than categorical grants, not only because of the possibility of attaching regulations to them but also because of the possibilities of expanding their audit provisions.

An equally important consideration concerns the reasons for wanting flexibility in the first place. One reason is economic, and this has to do with the belief that enabling the states and localities to sort out program commitments and combine program administration within broader areas will reduce administrative costs and free up more time that could be utilized more productively elsewhere. However, most observers seem to agree that these savings will be minimal when compared with the losses in state and local revenues resulting from congressionally approved budget cuts and the uncertainties of the second round of efforts yet to come.

The second reason for enhanced flexibility is the federalist principle. On this point, many of us share the vision of the day when the states can reassume their rightful place as full-fledged polities in the federal system, with the capacity to share the responsibilities of governance in ways that more closely reflect the preferences of their diverse publics. But the block grant approach is at best a halfway measure that must be continuously redirected toward that goal.

Sorting Out Functions in the Federal System

Throughout the post—World War II period there has been an unbroken series of efforts to sort out governmental functions in the federal system. First was the Hoover Commission on Executive Organization (1947–1949), followed by a second Hoover Commission (1953–1955), the Kestnbaum Commission on Intergovernmental Relations, the Joint Federal-State Action Committee in the late 1950s, various proposals of the U.S. Advisory Commission on Intergovernmental Relations, and others.

The latest in this series is the so-called "Alexander-Babbitt initiative," proposed by Republican Governor Lamar Alexander of Tennessee and Democratic Governor Bruce Babbitt of Arizona at the August 1981 meeting of the National Governors' Association in Atlantic City, New Jersey. As described by David Broder, the proposal essentially calls on the federal government to phase out aid to education and assume the state share of Medicaid (Broder and Naughtie 1981). Transportation and economic development aid would also be assumed by the states, according to B. Drummond Ayres, Jr. (1981).

While this proposal is intended to move beyond the "vague, woolly rhetoric" of federalism, as Governor Babbitt put it, there are several basic flaws in the idea of sorting out governmental functions. One is its allocation criterion, which would essentially place the entire responsibility for a particular function in the hands of whichever government is currently paying the most for it. This assumes, for example, that transferring Medicaid responsibilities to the federal government would somehow improve the administration of that program. In fact, such a transfer would accomplish little in and of itself save for increasing the pressures for a national bill to contain hospital costs.

A more basic problem with this approach is that it begins with the wrong question in formulating allocation criteria. As Martin Diamond (1969, p. 79) put it, "We should ask not what *is* local, but rather: by which level of government or combination of levels is it best that this or that thing be done?" Consider the case of education. We expect local authorities to operate elementary and secondary schools, because we believe that the way our children are taught should be a community responsibility. At the same time, we expect the states as polities to provide certain minimal standards having to do with the allocation of state education funds, requirements of teacher certification, standards of educational performance, and minimal curricular needs, though some states go so far as to dictate what textbooks should be used. At the same time, we expect the federal government to play a role, however minimal, in safeguarding the constitutional rights of students and teachers.

Another problem has to do with the assumptions of accountability built into this approach. Governor Alexander told the governors' conference that a sorting out of functions is needed "to make it clear to the taxpayer who is to blame if a program doesn't work." While there is no doubt that the present system obscures accountability, I am again unconvinced that the sorting out of functions is the answer. The citizen in a federal democracy also has certain federalist responsibilities, and one of those is becoming accustomed to following his or her interests and seeking redress in multiple arenas that often overlap.

At this point, I hasten to return to my central argument. The turning problem with the practice of federalism today is the lack of reservedness on the part of all governments in the federal system in their relations with each other and with the citizenry. In sorting out governmental responsibilities by functional areas, we run the risk of removing one of the last checks on governmental expansion and closing one of the final doors to the restoration of shared responsibilities. In this regard, my impatience with increased regulations in the name of power sharing is offset by my fear of the unchecked national centralization of welfare and, for that matter, the unchecked state centralization of education.

Turning Back Federal Revenues to State and Local Governments

On 30 June 1981 President Reagan told the National Conference of State Legislatures that "the ultimate objective ... is to use block grants as a bridge leading to the day when you will have not only the responsibility for programs that properly belong at the state level, but you'll have the tax sources now usurped by Washington returned to you—ending that round trip of the people's money to Washington and back minus a carrying charge."*

How will this be accomplished? Albert J. Davis and John Shannon (1981, p. 18) have suggested four basic alternatives for turning back federal revenues to state and local govern-

---

*As quoted in the *National Journal*, 22 August 1981, p. 1492.

ments: (1) revenue sharing on a formula basis, by which Congress, acting through the appropriations process, could substantially increase the present General Revenue Sharing Program or otherwise share its revenues with the states or with states and localities; (2) tax sharing on an origin basis, by which Congress could provide a state-local entitlement to a specific portion of tax receipts, with shares in the same proportion as tax revenues; (3) conditional relinquishment of a federal tax, by which Congress could give up part or all of a tax on the condition that the state or locality adopt that tax, for example, through a federal tax credit for state enactment of a "pick-up" tax; and (4) unconditional relinquishment of a federal tax, by which Congress could give up a portion of a tax or vacate an entire tax field without the requirement of a state or local "pickup."

These alternatives indicate both the compelling logic and potential controversies involved in the revenue turn-back idea. The logic rests on the basic idea that any transfer of responsibility back to the states and localities should be matched by a commensurate return of the funds needed to pay for it. If Congress were to relinquish an expenditure field unconditionally, presumably it would unconditionally relinquish a revenue field sufficient to pay for its adoption by states and localities. If Congress were to relinquish an expenditure field conditionally, presumably it would establish a conditional revenue transfer arrangement in which the conditions of the revenue "pickup" were commensurate with those of the responsibility transfer.

Unfortunately, the most relevant historical precedent was based on the premise that such a matching effort should follow up on a prior effort to sort out responsibilities by functional area—a premise with flaws, as I have already suggested. That example is the Joint Federal-State Action Committee, founded in 1957 by President Eisenhower, at a time when the mood of the country was not unlike today's. The committee was charged, first of all, "to designate functions which the States are ready and willing to assume and finance that are now performed or financed, wholly or in part by the federal government" (Grodzins 1966, p. 308). As committed as its members were to such an undertaking, the committee could identify only two such functions: vocational education and municipal waste treatment plants, together totaling $80 million in federal grants in 1957, or slightly more than 2 percent of all federal grants in that year. To pay for these programs, the committee recommended a federal tax credit for a state tax on local telephone calls, later modified in the name of equalization to guarantee every state at least 140 percent of what it was receiving at the time. Nothing ever came of the proposal, which quietly died in Congress.

Today the economic problem of inflation may make for a more receptive audience for such efforts, but the same basic issues remain unresolved. Would revenue turn-backs be based on the requirement of sorting out responsibilities by functional area or on a more careful determination of the reasons why a particular governmental plane or combination of planes should be involved in this or that function? Would the envisioned level of commitment by all governments be such that the existing rates of governmental spending—and hence, taxpayer burden—would simply be shifted from one plane to another, or would external incentive and replacement provisions enable a winding down of governmental spending? How would Congress be persuaded to free up more revenues than it now seems willing to do, or why should the states be asked to assume a tax that the federal government had relinquished? Finally, would the revenue turn-back be distributed according to returned responsibilities, need, or original contribution?

DEREGULATION AND THE IDEA OF LIMITED GOVERNMENT

It should be clear from the foregoing that no attempt to unwind the intergovernmental system can succeed without some prior commitment to unwind government itself. Clearly, intergovernmental relations are now big business, with federal grants alone totaling some $90 billion. But intergovernmental relations are, after all, only a product of the collective and individual decisions of governments; and these decisions, in turn, are products of the pressures on individual public officials and their preferences. Until those officials, on all planes of government, begin to reestablish reasonable limits on the role of government, the previously discussed efforts to unwind the intergovernmental system will appear to be little more than a shell game.

I do not have in mind any wholesale abdication of governmental responsibility. That would be both too easy and too much of a departure from the intent of the Framers and subsequent generations of federalists. Rather, I have in mind a restoration of commonsense notions of reasonableness and trust that are appropriate to the task of establishing the necessary and proper roles and the limits of government in our modern society. And this is a task that can be carried out only in the dirty and distracting trenches of the legislative and bureaucratic process. In every request for reauthorization, renewal, or new legislation, Congress and the president must apply not only economic but federalist principles to an assessment of whether the assumption of a new responsibility or the continuation of an existing one is really necessary or simply convenient. At the same time, state governors and legislatures must begin this reassessment process, for just as there are many federal programs and regulations that could more effectively be carried out by state and local governments or by no governments at all, there are many state programs and regulations that could more effectively be carried out by local governments or by no governments at all. Even local government could look to carefully deregulating its own house, beginning, if one were to follow Milton Friedman's advice, with taxicab medallions and rent controls (Friedman 1981, p. 58).

This is no easy task. But it is a time-honored one. As James Madison wrote (Hamilton, Madison, and Jay 1961, p. 322), "In framing a government which is to be administered by men over men, the great difficulty lies in this: you must first enable the government to control the governed; and in the next place, oblige it to control itself."

If recent court decisions are a guide, the robes of the U.S. Supreme Court will offer little protection to the self-controlling efforts of the political branches of government. In a string of federal regulatory cases in 1980–1981, the Supreme Court reaffirmed its commitment to defer to the executive and legislative branches in political decisions. In so doing, the Court, in this writer's opinion, properly gave Congress and the president ample scope. State interests fared variously in the process, on a case-by-case basis.

In the cases of *Hodel* v. *Indiana* and *Hodel* v. *Virginia Surface Mining and Reclamation Association,* the Court rejected the states' claim that the Surface Mining Control and Reclamation Act of 1977 unconstitutionally oversteps Congress's power to regulate commerce by imposing severe restrictions on land use, and thereby left it up to Interior Secretary James Watt and the House of Representatives to battle over cutting back the staff of the Office of Surface Mining. In *Harris* v. *McRae,* the Court upheld the limitations imposed by the Hyde amendment on federal funding of abortions and also indicated that nothing in Title XIX of the Social Security Act required states to make up the difference. This final point was reaffirmed in the Court's decision in *Williams* v. *Zbaraz,* which upheld the "little Hyde amendment" of Illinois. In July the Court affirmed the Montana State Supreme Court decision in *Commonwealth Edison* v. *Montana,* which upheld the state's coal severance tax and, by implication, the power of Congress to set reasonable limits to state severance taxes. However, in *Consolidated Freight-ways Corp. of Delaware* v. *Kassell,* a federal district court in Iowa overturned an Iowa statute prohibiting the use of 65-foot twin trailers on its highways. The statute was over-turned on the grounds that when a burdensome regulation cannot be said to make more than "the most speculative contribution to highway safety," it is unconstitutional.

In two other cases, the Court tightened the limits on state and local action from two different directions. In *Los Angeles* v. *Marshall,* the Supreme Court refused to review a U.S. Court of Appeals ruling that upheld a 1976 federal law re-quiring state and local government employees to be covered by unemployment insurance as a condition for state partic-ipation in the federal program for private employers. Along the way, the appeals court held that the county's argument based on the Tenth Amendment was invalid, because the federal program is technically voluntary. The Supreme Court in another case expanded the claims made against state and local officials on the basis of section 1983 of U.S.C. Title 42 (*Maine* v. *Thiboutot*). In short, even though states and local-ities continue to suffer setbacks to local control, the Court has left Congress and the president with as much leeway to cut back or share the regulatory burden as they have to ex-pand it.

Having suggested some of the fiscal and constitutional issues facing the American federal system, let me offer two general observations concerning the capacity of American institutions to respond to these issues. Nearly a century and a half ago, Alexis de Tocqueville (1969, p. 515) noted that "the more government takes the place of associations, the more will individuals lose the idea of forming associations and need government to come to their help."

The history of American institutions over the past fifteen

years proves Tocqueville's thesis only partially correct. The centralization of governmental institutions and the unparalleled expansion of their activities have engendered a commensurate centralization of political and civic institutions as they, in turn, have adapted and altered themselves to maintain access to government funding and public power. One sees this development not only in the internal organization and lobbying efforts of interest groups but also in the development throughout the 1970s of two national party committees as ongoing institutions. Leon D. Epstein (1981) has traced the different courses of this development in both major parties, focusing on the nationalizing tendencies of the Supreme Court's decisions regarding delegate selection questions in *Cousins* v. *Wigoda* and *Democratic Party of the U.S.* v. *La Follette*, and on the potentially federalist tendencies in the "grants-in-aid" method that has emerged within the Republican party "system."

At the same time, these and other developments have also strengthened the organizational capacity of governmental and nongovernmental institutions alike. One cannot say today, as one might have been able to say five years ago, that the institutional fabric of the American system is separating at the seams. Quite the contrary, America's representative institutions have never been stronger. State legislatures are taking a more active and recently legitimized role in the federal aid process. Many neighborhood associations and other voluntary organizations have been strengthened or formed as a result of the expansion of governmental assistance programs and the heightened political self-interests this has fostered. And partly because of the warnings of David Broder and others, one can no longer say about the two-party system that "the party's over."

In short, the institutional challenge facing the federal system in the 1980s is not what it was in the 1970s. For America's governmental, political, and civic institutions, the 1970s were a time of rebuilding; the 1980s should be a time of redirecting those institutions along federalist lines.

In sum, for institutional as well as economic and constitutional reasons, the path toward federalism is as unobstructed as it has ever been before or will be again. If we do not take this opportunity now, we will have lost the right to consider ourselves a federal people.

RESPONSES

F. Clifton White: "Defining the Conceptual Framework"

I think the resolution of the question of federalism is going to determine what kind of a society we are going to have for the rest of this century. Two very critical points lead us to the prospect of accomplishing some of the goals that Dr. Elazar and Dr. Schechter have outlined. First, there are basic, almost universal questions implied by Dr. Elazar and more specifically stated by Dr. Schechter: the people today are saying, "What the devil is government all about? Why do we have it? How much of it should we have? What should it do for us? Where should it be? How should it work?" Now, for political campaigns, we relate these questions back to a number of specific issues—taxes, welfare, etc.—that presumably translate into something the people can understand. This gives us a fertile field in which to try to give the general public an understanding of the discussions and dialogue in these two chapters.

The second point is that we now have a president dedicated to sorting out—or unwinding—our federal system. Ronald Reagan understands the conceptual framework of federalism, not as a catchword in a campaign, but as a concept for people to determine how they want their government to be run or what kind of government they want to have. Given that framework, it seems to me that we have a great opportunity to provide an intellectual backdrop of what the government is all about. There is a lot of work to do in defining what we are talking about in regard to federalism and the various areas in which federalism must apply if it is going to be effective. But now we have a basis for a real, effective, and practical dialogue about what it means to be a federalist country—about citizen responsibility and about the interrelationship of the citizen, his duties, and the government within a matrix system.

Alan F. Holmer: "Turning Away from Washington"

The foremost priority of this administration during its first six months was to achieve enactment of its economic package. But looking at the proposals contained in that package, one can see a federalist perspective everywhere. The budget cuts, for example, are designed to reorder priorities so that the national budget will address truly national needs. The block grants result from a major effort to consolidate categorical grant programs and reduce much of the regulatory overkill on the part of the federal government. And there have been a great many other regulatory relief actions, more than half of which came to the attention of this administration after concerns were expressed by state and local officials. Finally, the tax cuts have been focused on encouraging savings, investment, and productivity, in order to get the economic engine of our country moving again; but they also attack the problem of an oppressive level of federal taxation that in many instances has usurped revenue sources that otherwise might have been available to state and local governments.

Both Dr. Schechter and Dr. Elazar addressed the difference between a decentralized and a noncentralized government, and a few of Dr. Elazar's sentences go to the heart of the problem:

Noncentralization is not the same as decentralization. . . . Decentralization implies the existence of a central authority, a central government. The government that can *de*centralize can recentralize if it so desires. . . . In a noncentralized political system, power is so diffused that it cannot legitimately be centralized or concentrated without breaking the structure and spirit of the constitution.

When the president proposed a series of consolidations of categorical grants into block grants, he said that they would help make the government work again by decentralizing decision making in order to permit government decisions to be made by officials at the local level where they could be held accountable. He said that administrative savings would result from reducing the level of federal control or federal regulation—that it would permit experimentation on the part of the states and allow them once again to be true laboratories for democracy. He also argued that the reforms would reduce the impact of the budget cuts by permitting state and local officials to target diminishing resources to areas and individuals in greatest need. It is quite clear that the president appreciates the difference between decentralization and noncentralization. But he has also said that, as far as he is concerned, the block grants are only an interim step.

In addition to returning the authority and the responsibility for those block grants to the states, the president would like to return revenue sources to the states. Instead of taxing the states, sending the money to Washington, and then returning it to the states so they can administer the programs after a carrying charge has been deducted, we could leave the funds at the local level and local officials could make the decisions themselves.

Ronald Reagan is convinced that the steady flow of power and tax dollars to Washington, D.C., over the last several decades has helped create a situation where the government, at least at the federal level, just does not seem to work any more. It clearly is overloaded, having assumed far more responsibility than it can efficiently or effectively manage. One of the key causes of that governmental breakdown is the fact that policymakers have become less and less accountable to the voters as more and more decisions are made by officials in our nation's capital. It is far easier to hold an official accountable at a state or local level, when you can grab hold of him by the coat lapels or look him in the eye or knock on his door at home. There is not and never can be an equivalent degree of responsiveness on the part of federal officials.

To reach the goal of making government work again, public policy decisions have to be made with a few key questions clearly in mind. Is a given task the proper function for the government in the first place? Or can it be better handled by the private sector? The rebuttable presumption is that if there is a problem faced by our society, ideally it should be handled by the private sector. Once it has been determined that government involvement is required, one must ask—and ask honestly—if it is a proper function for the federal government to be involved in.

Steven Schechter made the point that up to now all eyes have looked to Washington. He is right. And this administration again has a rebuttable presumption that state or local responsibility is to be preferred. The assumption is that officials at the state and local level are every bit as competent, compassionate, and caring as officials in Washington, D.C. That is an assumption rejected by most of those who opposed the administration's block grant efforts. They felt the state and local officials really could not be counted upon to make the right decisions—a judgment that goes to the heart of any questions we have about returning power and authority to the state and local levels. More broadly, it goes to the heart of everything that Ronald Reagan and his administration stand for with respect to domestic affairs.

The president believes that simply working in Washington, D.C., does not give officials a corner on wisdom in this country. Just as economic decisions should be made in an unburdened economic marketplace, so too should political and governmental decisions be made in a free and open political process. Of course, there will be winners and there will be losers, but at least decisions should be made at a level where decision-makers can be held accountable for their actions.

One last point. Daniel Elazar mentioned that one of the first principles of federalism is that government should really involve a partnership and a spirit of cooperation among its various levels. As the president said in Atlanta in his speech to the National Conference of State Legislatures:

> The founding fathers saw the federal system constructed something like a masonry wall. The states are the bricks, the national government is the mortar. For the structure to stand plumb with the Constitution, there must be a proper mix of brick and mortar. Unfortunately, over the years, many people have come increasingly to believe that Washington is the whole wall, a wall that incidentally leans, sags, and bulges under its own weight.

Hence the president has placed a very high priority on establishing this spirit of cooperation. Partnership is not always easy in an era of diminishing resources, but it will continue to be a very high priority in this administration.

Paul Laxalt: "Reagan Federalism"

To begin the task of revitalizing our federal system, President Reagan has proposed the most sweeping realignment of government activities since the New Deal. The plan has two major components. Starting in fiscal 1984, the federal government will assume full responsibility for the cost of the expanding Medicaid program, in exchange for the states' picking up Aid to Families with Dependent Children (AFDC) and food stamps.

By assuming the whole governmental cost of health and virtually the entire financial responsibility for the elderly population, the federal government will be taking on the most rapidly growing domestic social needs.

The states will be picking up the areas where growth is much less rapid. Under current law, the total funding for AFDC and food stamps is projected to increase only 10 percent by 1987, compared with a projected 83 percent increase in the total cost of Medicaid for the same period.

The other aspect of the plan is a turn-back of responsibilities to the states for over forty federal programs in education, community development, transportation, and social services—along with the resources to pay for them. In 1984 the federal government will apply the full proceeds from certain excise taxes to a grass-roots trust fund that will belong in fair shares to the fifty states. By 1988 the states will be in complete control of these grant programs.

Now there are those who, for their own narrow political purposes, say the federalism plan is a mere diversion from our economic problems. Or that federalism is simply a means to cut the budget further. This is not the case. The president's federalism plan stands on its own merits, a key to a freer, better America. Federalism is too important an issue to be treated as a distraction, and the American people deserve a full and public debate of the proposal's merits.

Revitalizing the federal system requires an attack on a broad front. We have seen the first skirmishes of the battle in the block grant program and the administration's deregulation drive. Block grants were a major component of the president's economic recovery package. The proposal was simple: consolidate many categorical grants now supervised by thousands of federal employees and encumbered with enough red tape to sink a battleship into a few uncomplicated block grants relatively free of restriction or burdensome paperwork.

Today the duplication and waste in the categorical grant programs are nothing less than a managerial nightmare. In the area of health and social services, for example, the administration proposed consolidating thirty-nine federal categorical grants into block grants. Those categorical programs are now covered by over 400 pages of law and some 1,200 pages of regulation control for over 6,000 separate grants. Once awards are made, over 7 million man-hours of state and local government and community effort are used just in filling out the federally required reports each year. Presently it takes over 3,500 federal workers to manage $9 billion of these health and social service grants. The administration's proposal required only 160 federal workers and would put the people at the local level to work accomplishing their goals rather than filling out needless paperwork.

In education, the administration proposed consolidating forty-four separate federal elementary and secondary education programs into block grants. While there is little doubt that the present categorical program is based on good intentions, the effort to meet federal mandates at the local level draws increasing sums away from real services delivered to children into administration and other overhead costs that benefit no one. Furthermore, federal contributions, which are only 8 percent of total funds for education, have seriously distorted the division of responsibility of the American system. While the federal government contributes little, it controls much. Control of education was meant to be left with the states and the local community; it should be returned there as soon as possible.

Moreover, some local school employees are designing their systems not to meet local needs, but instead to comply with federal requirements. This undermines the interaction between parent and teacher, an important part of the education process. Simultaneously, there are complaints that federal administrators too often take an adversarial approach in their dealings with local school districts. Local needs and conditions are frequently excluded from discussion when it comes to determining whether the school has fully complied with the rigid and intricate guidelines cranked out of Washington. Yet there is really no reason to believe that parents and teachers have less concern about educa-

tional standards for their children than does the bureaucracy in Washington, D.C.

There was, undeniably, a dual purpose behind the block
grant program. Given that budget cuts would be necessary, it
was felt that, if more freedom and flexibility were given to
the states, it would be possible in many cases to maintain
nearly the same level of services while lowering the actual
number of tax dollars being spent. But just as important, the
Reagan administration believes that most of the programs
covered by its block grant proposals should be within the province of the states anyway, and that the block grant program is
a good first step in transferring total responsibility back to the
proper level of government.

The other half of the equation is the question of resources.
The president has stated on numerous occasions that he
would like to see revenue resources returned to the states as
well. Thus taxes that now go to Washington and then return
in the form of grants laden with red tape can, instead,
remain at the state and local levels, thus enabling state
and local governments to handle problems free of federal
interference.

Returning revenue sources to states and localities is one of
the major issues that the Presidential Advisory Committee
on Federalism is addressing. It strikes at the heart of the
problem: as long as the federal government is co-opting all of
the tax money, the states cannot be expected to assume their
rightful authority.

In 1819, Chief Justice of the Supreme Court John Marshall
likened the power to tax with the power to destroy. At the
present time, that is exactly what is happening. Not only is
excessive federal taxation destroying incentive and lowering
the standard of living of our individual citizens, but it is
destroying our federal system as well.

In the past year, the country has witnessed an epic battle
to redirect the course of American government. Spending
cuts were enacted that will save $130 billion over the next

three years. The American people won a tax cut that will leave $321 billion in their pockets in the next three years that would have been taxed away. These incredible pieces of legislation will have an impact on federalism, if for no other reason than that they leave more money at the local level and reverse a trend that saw federal power growing by leaps and bounds.

I am sad to say, however, that the block grant program was not as successful as it might have been. Powerful interest groups were able to blunt much of the effort. Nevertheless, it was—and this is important—just the first wave. And there was progress.

The Omnibus Budget Reconciliation Act of 1981, signed into law by the president on 13 August, did consolidate fifty-seven categorical grants into nine block grants. The new grants, most of which become effective in fiscal year 1982, are:

—Maternal and Child Health block grant, which consolidates seven categorical grants.

—Health Care and Preventive Health Services block grant, which consolidates eight categorical grants.

—Alcohol, Drug Abuse, and Mental Health block grants, which consolidate five categorical grants.

—Primary Care block grant, which converts the categorical community health centers program into a block grant.

—Social Services block grant, which consolidates more than $2.5 billion in federal Title XX social services programs, including child day care, homemakers' services, social services, training, and others.

—Low Income Energy Assistance.

—Community Services Administration block grant, which is a program to replace the Community Services Administration.

—Education block grant, which simplifies and consolidates federal elementary and secondary education programs.

Some of these block grants did not go as far at eliminating the red tape and federal controls as we would have liked. However, this was just the first wave. In the years ahead we expect to expand the block grant concept, including more federal programs and decreasing the red tape on those already functioning, while at the same time returning the revenue sources to the states.

The block grant program is just one part of Reagan federalism. Another part is the deregulation campaign now under the personal direction of Vice-President Bush. The campaign affects a cross section of American industry as well as state and local governments. The departments and agencies are taking the effort seriously, as is reflected in the dramatic decrease in the number of pages in the *Federal Register*, a book listing all new regulations. It appears that the bureaucratic rule making in the final year of the previous administration will have taken up 50 percent more pages in the *Federal Register* than regulations brought into line during President Reagan's first twelve months.

A major part of the deregulation drive is specifically aimed at getting Washington regulators off the backs of state and local governments. Some of what has already been done to reduce overhead costs and return decision making to the state and local levels can be seen in the efforts undertaken to streamline Medicaid regulations affecting the states and to return regulation of pesticides to local authorities. In addition, the new administration has:

—Withdrawn proposed bilingual education rules, which will save up to $1 billion per year.

—Withdrawn a policy memorandum establishing federal review of certain hospital construction.

—Withdrawn standby energy conservation measures.

The depth of the Reagan administration's commitment to federalism extends far beyond block grants and regulatory reform. It often takes the form of increased sensitivity and awareness of the state and local governments' needs and strengths; such a change in attitude is difficult to quantify but of immense practical importance. Other aspects of the pursuit of federalism are significant and easily measured actions, such as dismantling one of the major vehicles for federal usurpation: the Department of Education.

The following are some examples of federal department or agency actions that promote a strong federal system.

—The federal Office of Surface Mining in the Department of Interior has been reorganized, so the federal government's role will be to give assistance and advice, as well as to review state efforts.

—The secretary of the interior has frequently referred to federal adoption of a "good neighbor policy." A practical example is the federal government's willingness to swap land holdings of equal value to enable states to develop contiguous holdings and thus more efficiently utilize state lands.

—The Department of Health and Human Services intends to strengthen and free the regional offices to assume greater responsibility.

—The Department of Housing and Urban Development is developing an urban policy that will be oriented toward greater local involvement. A particular virtue of such an approach is the flexibility to experiment. The Urban Enterprise Zone is a concept totally compatible with the goals of Reagan federalism and worth a try.

What has happened in Washington is nothing less than a revolution. The country was headed toward a centralization of power totally inconsistent with American tradition. Yet since the inauguration of President Reagan we have made progress that a short time ago was considered impossible.

Finally, we should consider for a moment the opponents of Reagan federalism. There are, of course, those whose pocketbooks are tied into the status quo. Even if it meant economic catastrophe for the country, these people would oppose change because they would be making money even as the ship was sinking. But there are others—sincere people—who simply do not trust state and local government. They recoil at such phrases as "states' rights," and for a good reason.

Even those of us who are ardent supporters of Reagan federalism must admit that for many years many who talked about the importance of states' rights were actually using the concept as a cover to protect brutal and racist laws—laws that were a disgrace to our nation.

But to relate the separation of power to the protection of bigotry is a serious mistake. We have smashed laws that discriminate on account of race. Furthermore, civil rights guarantees will remain untouched by any block grant proposals.

Opposing Reagan federalism out of fear of racism in the states is living in the past. And while discrimination will be struck down if it raises its ugly head again, we must move forward and correct the problems of today—problems that for the most part stem from an imbalance of governmental power.

Today it is in the interest of every citizen to eliminate the waste, inefficiency, and arrogance associated with the centralization of power.

The growth of federal power has spread an oppressive haze over this country. It smothers the incentive of our people and chokes the vitality of the nation. It has nearly destroyed the confidence that once was the hallmark of America.

Our system of government is unique among nations. It encompasses checks and balances, a separation of powers, and the protection of inalienable rights.

In recent years this beautiful jewel, handed from generation to generation, has been distorted almost beyond recognition. It is our task today to restore that system—the American system—which has provided us with the greatest personal freedom, political liberty, and material abundance the world has ever known.

III

The Reagan Administration's Federalism Policy Proposals

5

MURRAY L. WEIDENBAUM*

Strengthening Our Federal System

The loss of state autonomy. "Free" federal assistance. The Reagan program. A shift in federal priorities. Regulatory reform. Private business. The need for diversity.

The Reagan administration is dedicated to strengthening our federal system of government. Issues of federalism are at the heart of our efforts to preserve liberty, draw strength from our regional diversity, and accommodate the realities of efficiently providing a wide variety of governmental services.

*Reprinted from the *Journal of Contemporary Studies* 4, 4 (Fall 1981), pp. 71–77.

But while issues of federalism are always important, I suggest that they are especially important today for two major —and different—reasons.

THE NATURE OF THE PROBLEM

First, by a federal system we mean the concurrent existence of
a strong central government and similarly strong and independent state governments. But in the past decade we have
seen a boom in federal social regulation with devastating consequences for the federal system. By what lawyers and political scientists call "supersession," the federal government,
through many of its regulatory actions, has reduced the
autonomy of state governments and centralized the responsibilities for many important social, economic, and regulatory
programs. This loss of autonomy has weakened the states and
reduced their independence, while the centralization of
responsibilities better handled at state and local levels has
limited the effectiveness of the federal government.

I am not alone in this opinion. Following a three-year study
undertaken at the request of Congress, the Advisory Commission on Intergovernmental Relations (ACIR) reached the
disturbing conclusion that American federalism is in serious
trouble. I quote from their December 1980 report: "The
federal government's influence ... has become more pervasive, more intrusive, more unmanageable, more ineffective, more costly, and above all, more unaccountable."

In making this uncomplimentary observation, ACIR has
estimated that 1,259 federal regulations have been imposed
on state and local governments. Of these, 223 were direct orders and the remaining 1,036 were conditions of aid. Fifty-
nine of these requirements were so-called "crosscutting"
rules that applied to virtually all federal grants.

In a recent study of six federal regulatory programs in

seven U.S. cities, researchers at the Urban Institute in Washington, D.C., concluded that complying with federal rules cost these city governments an average $24 per capita (or $96 for a typical family of four). These figures, of course, exclude the costs of the multitude of other regulations that fall on municipal governments plus all of the regulations affecting states.

The second reason for the present concern over the future of the federal system is that, through well-intentioned federal financing of many state and local government programs, the federal government has inadvertently eroded state authority by creating a degrading dependence of state and local authorities on so-called "free" federal money.

By 1980 there were nearly 500 intergovernmental grants-in-aid programs. Each of these has its own restrictions and its own auditing and reporting requirements that pile red tape upon red tape. Further, many of the programs overlap. In 1978, for example, thirty-five programs existed for pollution control and abatement, seventy for secondary and vocational education, and thirteen for conservation and land management.

When we look at this phenomenon from the other end of the federal system, the results are appalling. A recent *Washington Post* series entitled "Appleton: A Regulated City" gave those of us in Washington who deal with regulation a taste of its effects from the receiving end. Over one hundred federal agencies regulate different aspects of life in Appleton, Wisconsin—a prosperous town of about 60,000 people. While the residents of Appleton realize that some federal regulations have improved the quality of their lives and are necessary, they also have many "horror stories" to tell. Among these is the $4,000 wheelchair lift in a building at Lawrence University—built to comply with federal rules but used only once since 1978. Or the ten months that the local radio station, WROE–FM, has been waiting for federal approval of a routine one-day repair job on its antenna.

THE REAGAN ADMINISTRATION'S
EFFORTS FOR CHANGE

The Reagan administration is unquestionably committed to restoring and strengthening the federal system. As President Reagan noted in his inaugural address, the state governments created the federal governments and not the other way around. The president has reaffirmed his administration's commitment to restoring a proper balance in government, not only in words but in actions. He also has established a Presidential Advisory Committee on Federalism, chaired by Senator Paul Laxalt, to inform and advise the administration on the wide range of issues encompassed by federalism.

The Reagan administration is dedicated to reversing the trend towards greater control over state and local programs by the federal government. Our approach can be summarized by the following guiding principles:

- Substitute, to the maximum extent possible, state for federal government in dealing with local governments.

- Substitute state and local governments for the federal government in dealing with private institutions and individual citizens.

- Cap open-ended federal matching programs.

- Combine and move to the states (and localities) categorical federal programs through a block grant process.

- Provide maximum state discretion and minimum federal constraints in all block grants.

- Place planning, audit, and review functions at the state level, utilizing regular state agencies wherever possible.

- Move regulatory authority from the federal to the state level of government where such shifts are appropriate.

- Remove to the extent possible spending mandates on state and local governments from federally financed programs.

- Give serious examination to replacing federal funding with a movement of revenue sources from the federal government to state and local governments.

Consider the president's economic recovery program. Each of its parts is a critical element in the restoration of a strong federal system.

The president's budget proposals, for example, included the consolidation of literally scores of categorical grant programs into a comprehensive system of block grants. Block grants not only reduce the overhead burdens on all levels of government, but more important, they return discretion and accountability over expenditures to state and local authorities. Congress has taken some initial steps to create several block grants, but more needs to be accomplished in the future.

A good example of the intent of this change is the educational block grant. It gives the states over $4 billion for fiscal years 1982 through 1984 to cover over twenty-five separate and narrow programs that existed previously. In the future, specific educational needs and priorities will be determined by state and local educational agencies.

The administration's budget also reflects a shift in federal priorities to truly national needs. Both national defense and an adequate "social safety net" for the truly needy are national priorities and federal responsibilities. On the other hand, many of the cuts in federal programs reflect both their ineffectiveness and the fact that the federal budget cannot accommodate the wishes of every economic or social group in the nation.

POLICY ACTIONS

Our policy of regulatory reform is designed to strengthen the federal system. The elimination of ineffective regulations and insistence on sound justification for all regulatory actions will substantially reduce burdens on state and local budgets. These public institutions, like their private sector counterparts, have seen their costs rise uncontrollably in recent years due to excessive federal regulatory requirements, and our policy of regulatory reform has already started to correct this problem. For example:

• The secretary of education has withdrawn proposed rules that would have required all school systems to offer a particular form of bilingual instruction to children whose primary language is other than English, at an estimated cost of up to $1 billion over the first five years and between $72 and $157 million a year thereafter.

• The secretary of education has proposed canceling a regulation dealing with public school dress codes.

• The Department of Transportation has delayed four regulations that would have imposed costly requirements on state and local governments, dictating how they conduct urban transportation planning, design traffic control devices, and rehabilitate or stockpile buses purchased with federal aid.

• The Treasury Department has postponed for reconsideration rules that would have imposed extensive new obligations on local governments that receive revenue-sharing funds to prevent discrimination against the handicapped in services, employment, and access to facilities.

Another case of relief for a classic example of overzealous regulation concerns garbage trucks. The Environmental Protection Agency (EPA) requested the D.C. Court of Appeals to remand to it for reconsideration a rule the agency had issued setting noise emissions standards for garbage trucks. This rule was not among EPA's most costly: about $25 million a year would have been required to bring garbage trucks into compliance. But these costs, however modest, would have been paid by financially hard-pressed municipalities.

More important, garbage truck noise is a prime example of a problem where there is no compelling reason for federal intervention. Garbage truck noise is a local problem whose severity varies from city to city. Local governments should be responsible for determining what, if anything, to do about it. Moreover, they should have flexibility in deciding how to respond. For example, altering truck routes and schedules to avoid residential neighborhoods in the early morning hours may be a better and cheaper solution in many cities than ordering expensive soundproofed trucks, as the EPA rule would have required nationwide.

And these examples are only part of what we have done. In all, this administration has already taken over one hundred separate actions aimed at reducing the burden of regulations on our citizens. At least thirty-four of these actions, including those I cited earlier, reduce the overhead costs on state and local governments and return decision making to state and local levels. They include changes in the following areas:

- Medicaid regulations affecting states.

- Pesticide regulations to meet local needs.

- Revenue-sharing/handicapped-discrimination regulations.

- Emergency stockpiling of buses,

- Elimination of the high-altitude requirements on 1984-model cars.

- Supersession of state energy efficiency standards for appliances.

It is obvious from these examples that regulatory reform will reduce overhead costs and increase the efficiency of state and local governments. But I would also stress that in the spirit of a truly federal system this administration's policy of regulatory relief will increase the discretion—and the responsibility—of state and local governments.

The economic policies of this administration are designed to be a coherent package; they will go a long way toward restoring the balance of power among governmental units in the United States. However, still more can be done to implement the administration's commitment to strengthening the federal system.

For one thing, we will resist budgetary actions that decrease grants to state and local governments unless there are corresponding decreases in the regulatory manacles that bind the hands of local officials and raise their costs.

Second, we will expect that any demand by the federal government on its partners in the federal system be backed up with the revenue to meet that demand. This will require any proposed legislation that might force costs on the states to be supported by analysis of just how much it would cost them if approved. Similarly, we have task forces studying the desirability of shifting expenditure responsibilities *and* tax powers to the states, where that would be a more appropriate division of labor.

While we all know that analysis alone never dictates legislative decisions, I am convinced that much of the past erosion of state and local authority was unintentional, and that the mere recognition of the extent of the problem will contribute to its solution.

Let me try briefly to cover a topic of some complexity: the relationship between strengthening the federal system and promoting a strong business system. Private business traditionally supports efforts to reduce federal taxing and federal spending. But often the business response is more ambiguous in the regulatory arena. To be sure, attempts to reduce federal regulation are often (but not universally) encouraged. Yet shifting regulatory responsibilities to states and localities is rarely welcomed by business because of its concern over the diversity of regulatory requirements, restraints, and prohibitions that can result.

In my view, the answer is not to centralize regulatory responsibilities. Rather, state governments themselves have the opportunity to distinguish between the areas where diversity is appropriate and those where standardization is suggested. Indeed, that is already done in many instances. For example, the states have developed, on their own, uniform codes of commercial conduct that are in general use in the United States.

Of course, I should hope that our program of regulatory relief encourages state and local governments to emulate our efforts. If there is anything that we have learned from our studies of government regulation over the years, it is the need to restrain—and not to encourage—the regulatory reflex on the part of government at all levels.

THE NEED FOR DIVERSITY

Finally, I believe there is one other very basic action we can take that will simultaneously reinvigorate the federal system and use it to full advantage. We must come to recognize the growing need for a "portfolio" or diversification approach to an increasing number of our economic, regulatory, and social problems.

An investor who is smart enough to see the financial opportunities associated with investments in, say, the electronics industry is also usually smart enough to know that only by luck will he or she actually be able to identify the individual companies that will profit most from these opportunities. Consequently, the investor chooses a portfolio of investments, some of which win and some of which lose. On average, however, the financial returns tend to be good because the commitment has been not to the common stock of a single firm but to a portfolio of investment instruments representing a large number of different companies.

As policymakers at the federal level, we often identify a real social or regulatory problem, but then foolishly commit ourselves to a single course of action—much as if we were an investor committed to a single common stock.

Not only is such a commitment unduly presumptuous of our own ability to pick the right solution the first time, it is also unduly risky—and, within a federal system, quite unnecessary. Independent actions by strong state and local governments on complex social issues can represent an ideal way to "diversify" the nation's portfolio of policy actions. The decisions by some state banking authorities to authorize variable interest rate mortgages were good examples of such state-level policy innovations that later were adopted at a national level.

We have a federal system of government that is, in effect, a portfolio designed by the framers of our Constitution, which could provide the advantages of diversification if allowed to work. As we attempt to restore the balance among governmental units that we have inadvertently lost, let us not settle for too little. There are simply too many opportunities to strengthen the federal system in ways that will allow us to exploit fully the distinctive competence of every level of government for the mutual benefit of the citizenry as a whole.

6

RICHARD S. WILLIAMSON

A Review of
Reagan Federalism

The administration and state flexibility in spending decisions. Block grants. Tax cuts. New presidential groups on regulatory relief, intergovernmental relations, and federalism. Response to the power shift.

President Reagan presented his New Federalism proposals to the American people nearly a year after the formulation of his original economic package. The interval between the presentation of these two initiatives has tended to obscure the deep connection between them. What is often unnoticed is that three of the four key components of the original package—budget cuts, regulatory relief, and tax cuts— directly reflected the president's perspectives on federalism.

These early economic initiatives were in fact federalist in design. From the beginning, the president has shaped a coherent structure within which his administration can address federalism issues.

BUDGET CUTS

A first major step in the return of authority and revenue sources to state and local governments is to cut the federal government itself. President Reagan's budget proposals meant a dramatic shift in the growth of government.

In March 1981 the president made the following remarks about his proposed budget cuts to the National League of Cities:[1]

I know that accepting responsibility, especially for cutbacks, is not easy. But this package should be looked at by state and local governments as a great step toward not only getting America moving again, but toward restructuring the power system which led to the economic stagnation and urban deterioration.

And the president said before another forum the same month:[2]

We are not cutting the budget simply for the sake of sounder financial management. This is only a first step toward returning power to states and communities, only a first step toward reordering the relationship between citizen and government.

President Reagan's federalist principles were evident throughout the many budget proposals that he submitted to Congress on 10 March 1981. The cuts in the urban mass transit operating assistance, to be phased out beginning in 1983, and in secondary and urban highway systems, to be phased out beginning in 1982, are justified on the basis that these functions more properly belong in the province of state and local governments.

One of the most significant proposals was for a 5 percent interim cap on the growth of federal matching payments for Medicaid while permanent fundamental reforms are being developed. (In later years the proposed cap would have been limited to the percentage increase in the gross national product [GNP] deflator.) The intent was to greatly enhance state flexibility and permit states to pursue efficiency in other ways. Currently, states lack the incentives—and in some cases the flexibility—to take advantage of economies of scale or competitive bidding in purchases and are often unduly constrained in contractual agreements. The president's overall purpose throughout the budget proposals was to provide local government more control over spending decisions.

The president's efforts to cap Medicaid did not pass Congress. However, he did succeed in giving the states much of the flexibility they needed for designing their own Medicaid systems. While not all aspects of his sweeping budget proposals passed Congress, aggregate cuts of approximately $37 billion for fiscal year 1982 have been signed into law (Public Law 97–35).

Among the most dramatic proposals were President Reagan's efforts to consolidate literally scores of categorical grants into block grants. Block grants are intended to restore authority to the state and local governments, maximize state and local discretion, and ultimately eliminate all central government control over the programs in the block grant through a shift in tax sources.

The system that developed over the years of allocating federal funds to state and local areas was organized into a myriad of specific categorical grants serving narrowly defined groups. This system has become a confusing tangle of small programs that overlap, conflict, and over-regulate. Categorical grants have systematically taken discretionary authority away from state and local officials, transforming them into mere administrators of federal programs. And the growth and proliferation of these categorical grants have been dramatic.

In 1959 total federal spending for some forty grants-in-aid programs was $6.7 billion, accounting for 1.4 percent of the GNP. By 1970 there were 130 categorical grant programs, and by 1980 the number stood at 492; total federal spending had skyrocketed to about $90 billion, a 1,243 percent increase since 1959, accounting for 3.3 percent of GNP. Furthermore, the categorical grant programs in 1959 dealt principally with transportation and income security. By 1978 the 492 federal grants-in-aid programs covered virtually every facet of state and local government.

President Reagan proposed the consolidation of eighty-eight categorical grants into seven block grants covering health, education, and social services. Sixty-three of the programs are currently funded at under $100 million annually, with thirty of these spending less than $10 million.

These Reagan block grant proposals represented the most far-reaching effort ever attempted in the consolidation of federal grants-in-aid programs. Only five block grants had been enacted out of approximately twenty proposed over the last two decades: Title XX of the Social Security Act, the Comprehensive Employment and Training Act, the Law Enforcement Assistance Act, the Community Development block grant, and the Partnership for Health. But none of these initiatives had fully relieved state and local officials from the burden of federal strings.

Although the president's proposals did not pass Congress in their entirety, he did achieve substantial and unprecedented success: fifty-seven former categorical programs have been combined into nine new or changed block grants with budget authority of over $13.6 billion.

REGULATORY REFORM

Reagan federalism also involves providing state and local governments with significant regulatory reform. As President Reagan has said, "In the last decade . . . local government has had to deal with an avalanche of federal regulation."[3] Just as consolidating categorical into block grants enhances efficiency and accountability, so does devolving certain regulations from the federal to the state and local levels. Each locality can establish standards consistent with environmental, economic, and social preferences.

In the opening days of his administration, the president announced a Presidential Task Force on Regulatory Relief, chaired by Vice-President George Bush.[4] The vice-president solicited input to this task force from a wide spectrum of individuals and organizations, including many state and local officials who contributed over two hundred submissions identifying over five hundred regulations for review. This review process has begun with the aid of the Office of Management and Budget (OMB). Under review is a cost-benefit analysis not only of how regulations might affect the private sector but also of their cost impact on state and local governments (Executive Order No. 12291, 17 February 1981).

This cabinet-level task force took 108 regulatory relief actions in the first hundred days of the Reagan administration. Thirty-four of these initiatives reduce the impact of regulation on state and local governments. Furthermore, Vice-President Bush on 12 August 1981 announced at a press conference thirty further regulatory relief actions, eighteen of which benefit state and local governments.

TAX CUTS

President Reagan also is committed to helping state and local governments by returning meaningful revenue sources to them. The president's dramatic "5–10–10" cut in marginal tax rates will allow more money to be available for state and local governments. For example, in California alone, the recently enacted federal tax cut will—over the next three years—leave more than $38.5 billion in the hands of Californians to spend as they wish. This decrease in taxes will stimulate economic growth and decrease the percentage of an earner's money taken by the federal government. The result is a greater tax base for state and local governments.

Also, the president has established a Cabinet Council work group under Secretary of the Treasury Donald Regan to examine the issues of revenue source return to state and local governments. This group is investigating certain federal excise taxes, federal revenue sharing, and other vehicles to return further revenues.

ESTABLISHING A STRUCTURE FOR FEDERALISM

President Reagan has asked all cabinet members to ensure that there is a high-level person with responsibility for intergovernmental affairs in each of their respective departments or agencies. He has instructed cabinet members to conduct "early and genuine consultations" with state and local officials concerning program and policy changes. And he has called on them to monitor programs carefully to ensure that they do not have unintended and undesirable effects on state and local governments.

For the first time in many years, the executive branch is participating actively in the Advisory Commission on Intergovernmental Relations (ACIR), which has provided a valuable resource for state and local governments but has too often been ignored by the executive branch. For only the second time in its history, ACIR is now chaired by an executive branch member, Secretary of the Interior James Watt.

The president has also appointed a Presidential Advisory Committee on Federalism chaired by U.S. Senator Paul

Laxalt, whose experience in local and state government and in the U.S. Senate provides him a unique position from which to address many issues of federalism. The committee has reached out to state legislators, governors, mayors, county officials, members of Congress, and private citizens to join in this forum to replenish the intellectual capital of federalism and to give specific guidance on programs the administration is addressing.

President Reagan has also devoted a great deal of personal time to consulting with state and local officials. In his first six months in office, along with addressing the annual meetings of the National Conference of State Legislatures and the National League of Cities, the president met with over 1,200 state and local officials in the White House.

In addition to the initiatives noted above, each of the federal departments and agencies has taken major steps to return authority and responsibility to state and local governments. From the Interior Department's swapping of its lands with those of western states, to the transfer of surplus federal property to the states for use as prison facilities, and even to the nomination of Sandra Day O'Connor to the Supreme Court—the first justice chosen from state government in over a quarter century[5]—the president's "quiet federalist revolution" is well under way.

POLITICAL REALITIES

The current redefining and correcting of our federalism system are fundamental to how our intergovernmental system will function for years to come. And as in the case of any historic shift of power—in this case from the central government to its appropriate place with state and local governments—the political crosscurrents are strong.

There is no question that critical to the success of the

president's Economic Recovery Program in Congress was the strong support given by the National Governors' Association (NGA), the National Conference of State Legislatures (NCSL), and the National Association of Towns and Townships (NATaT); the qualified support of the National Association of Counties (NACO) and the National League of Cities (NLC); and the divided signals of the U.S. Conference of Mayors. These public interest groups were willing to continue a constructive dialogue throughout the congressional deliberations on the budget proposals. And some of these groups—NGA, NCSL, and NATaT—forged a strong activist partnership with the administration. Then–NGA chairman Governor George Busbee reported that the nation's governors would actively support the proposed budget cuts in exchange for the flexibility provided in the proposed block grants. He went on to say that they gave this support with some hesitancy. They feared they might get the cuts but not the block grants.

The president assured the governors that he would fight with equal determination for both the block grants and the budget cuts; that he supported block grants above and beyond any budgetary considerations; and that he supported the grants as an interim step in achieving his dream for a New Federalism.[6]

The NGA and NCSL promised to help the president battle the "iron triangle"[7] for the budget cuts in exchange for a pledge that he would fight equally hard for block grants. It was a deal the president gladly embraced. And, importantly, it was a bipartisan coalition. Both NGA and NCSL are composed of more elected Democrats than Republicans, and that grass-roots Democratic leadership would prove crucial in helping the president get his program through the Democrat-controlled House.

Local government leaders were more reluctant to support the president's program. They were especially concerned that the president intended to dramatically cut or even entirely eliminate the federal government's relationship with local governments (see Viscount and Jordan 1981). Most local governments, especially big-city mayors, had developed federal grantsmanship to a high art form. They had far more success in getting funding aid directly from the federal government than from their own state capitols. The local officials, especially urban county officials and mayors of larger cities, felt state governments had been unfair in distribution of state monies, favoring rural over urban areas.[8] They believed the federal government had been a valuable ally in correcting this unfairness.

Also, mayors and county officials questioned the capacity of state governments to effectively handle the added responsibilities consequent to the Reagan budget proposals. As Mayor Charles Royer of Seattle charged, states are "politically, institutionally, and financially ill-equipped to assume added responsibilities of the magnitude contemplated in President Reagan's recovery program."[9]

Nonetheless, local officials appreciated the momentum of a new president and the deep commitment of Ronald Reagan to get his budget cuts. Consequently, their national organizations gave the president qualified support, and many of them became active lobbyists for the president's program. For example, the U.S. Conference of Mayors, composed of the big-city mayors, had a record going back thirty years of always asking the federal government for more money. A strong majority of their membership is Democratic. It was from among the ranks of this organization that President Carter had received his strongest support. Even though their national president, Mayor Richard Hatcher of Gary, Indiana, was a vice-chairman of the Democratic National Committee, the U.S. Conference of Mayors altered directions in 1981.

After their annual convention in Louisville, Kentucky, in June, Republican mayors, joined by conservative and moderate Democratic mayors from the Sun Belt, muted criticism of the president. Instead of expanded financing, the resolutions adopted typically called for a continuation of current funding. On a few points, wording that called for restoring cuts was dropped. Thus while the conference was not a partner with the president in his campaign for budget cuts, it was neutralized.

The support of local and state officials for the president's budget cut proposals was particularly important because it is these officials who deliver most of the people-related services that were to be cut. Their support for the overall package and willingness to absorb the cuts if given greater flexibility muted a significant dimension of potential criticism to the proposals.

The active lobbying of these political leaders was extremely helpful. Each was a community leader with his or her own political machinery: precinct workers, media liaisons, or volunteer organizations. When these officials spoke out in support of the president's program at home in Washington, members of Congress heard their voices.

In the end, the battle of the budget shifted for state and local officials from the size of the cuts to the block grants and the Medicaid cap. The president wanted his block grants and a Medicaid cap; state and local officials were strong supporters of the block grants and able adversaries against a Medicaid cap.

From the outset, the governors and state legislators were strong supporters of the block grants, which they saw as a means of gaining more control, increased flexibility, and administrative efficiency. Local officials also had records of calling for consolidation of categorical grants into blocks, but they feared an arbitrary transfer of federal mandates for state mandates. Further, there was a heavy atmosphere of distrust between state and local officials.

Liberals who opposed the cuts and block grants, both among state and local officials and in Congress, seized this opening. They argued that local governments that had suffered under the arbitrary and often heavy hand of federal bureaucrats with categorical grants would now be afflicted by the worse fate of arbitrary state mandates administered by state legislatures and state bureaucrats who were incompetent, had a heavy rural bias, and were even more susceptible to special interest lobbying than officials in Washington. Consequently, the initial political alliances were the administration and state government officials versus local officials, the iron triangle, and the Democrat-controlled House.

The administration felt that if the true nature of the proposed block grants would be explained, most of the opposition from local governments would disappear. The success of its "education" campaign became evident as more and more local officials backed off their criticism of the proposals.

During the home stretch of congressional deliberations, state and local officials in near unanimity supported the president's block grant proposals. The vested special interest groups, some turf-conscious congressmen, and some members of Congress who sincerely have little faith in state and local governments, did succeed in watering down the president's proposals. Some categoricals escaped consolidation. Some block grants were encumbered with earmarks. But nonetheless, Congress gave President Reagan's federalism initiatives a great victory in consolidating fifty-seven categorical grants into blocks. As NGA said about these block grant victories:[10]

Seven months after taking office, President Reagan has changed the direction of a federal aid system.... It represents some progress toward greater flexibility for state and local officials at a time when aid to state and local governments is shrinking.

And the president has pledged that he will "go back and back and back again" to Congress to get the flexibility for state and local governments denied them by Congress and to get further block grants.

Just as President Reagan's budget and block grant victories showed the beneficial political leverage of a union with state and local officials, the defeat of the president's pro-

posed Medicaid cap is a warning of potential roadblocks from
unified state and local opposition to a presidential proposal.

From the outset, there was strong opposition to the Medicaid cap proposal; NGA, NCSL, and NACO were especially
forceful in their objections. No compromise could be reached.
State and local officials, under the effective leadership of
Governor George Busbee, lobbied vigorously against the cap,
and it was defeated by Congress.

SUMMARY

President Reagan is deeply committed to the quiet revolution
of a New Federalism—returning the constitutional balance
whereby there is forged a meaningful "partnership" between
the federal, state, and local governments. Overall, he has
achieved substantial early success. But efforts to realize
further devolution will require reforming time and again the
political alliance of state and local officials with the administration to wage political battle against the iron triangle.

Already there are strains. The president was more successful in winning budget cuts than in achieving all the flexibility he sought in block grants. And the serious economic
problems we face require President Reagan to seek even
deeper cuts in federal spending.

One commentator has said that the governors have their
fingers crossed; so, too, do their fellow state and local officials
(Broder 1981). While most can agree on the ultimate objectives of more responsibility, authority, and revenue sources
at the state and local levels, the ways and means will be
precarious—forcing the administration to redouble its
efforts to insure that these early positive federalism steps
are not aberrations but a prelude to reforming our intergovernmental system, to correcting the existing imbalance,
to again making government work.

RESPONSES

Eugene Eidenberg: "Federalism: A Democratic View"

Over thirty years ago Franklin Roosevelt said:

If we limit government to the functions of merely punishing the criminal after crimes have been committed, of gathering up the wreckage of society after the devastation of an economic collapse, or fighting a war that reason might have prevented, then government fails to satisfy those urgent human purposes which, in essence, gave it its beginning and provide its present justification.

Not since the time of Roosevelt has the question of the role and effectiveness of government been more central in our national debate. In examining the "New Federalism," the question is whether there is a coherent philosophy guiding the Reagan administration's proposals for reallocating power and authority among different levels of government. Is the driving force the president's long-held view that the federal government has become too big, that its regulatory presence with respect to state and local government has grown cumbersome and unmanageable, and that to improve the effectiveness of government we must devolve responsibilities to the state and local levels? Or is the New Federalism yet another expression of the president's desire to shrink the size of government by reducing federal spending without regard to the logic or consequence of the reductions?

It is hard for me, on the basis of the administration's statements and actions thus far, to know with certainty which concerns are operating here. But, on balance, I have concluded that the driving force behind the administration's decisions about federalism is primarily a concern with the federal deficit—a concern with implementing certain budgetary policies and tax proposals. As a result, in my view, some fundamental questions concerning our federal system and efficient government have been either skipped over too lightly or ignored altogether. If the New Federalism is enacted into law as proposed, governors, state legislators, county supervisors, mayors, and other elected officials at the state and local levels will be living with the consequences of what are in fact basic economic policy decisions presented in the guise of decisions about federalism. In short, at the bottom of the New Federalism is, I believe, the administration's belief that the best way to cut spending is to eliminate the substantial support that the federal government currently provides for a variety of programs administered by state and local governments.

If we are going to address responsibly the question of the relationships among federal, state, and local governments and answer the most basic questions citizens can ask in a democratic society, we need to ask: What services do we, as a society, want government to provide? And what level of government can best provide them? What revenue source should be used to finance these services? Take the most obvious cases. Garbage collection, police protection, and fire protection are clearly services we want local government to provide. National defense is a federal concern. But between these two polar extremes there is a virtual infinity of choices that a democratic society has before it at any given time. Before the national government preemptively decides, in the name of fiscal austerity, that it is going to cut 30 percent and more from the revenues that now support services at the state and local level and fundamentally restructure management control over them, these prior questions must be addressed.

I do not approach this problem with an unqualified belief

that the federal government has all the answers, that it is necessarily the most effective level of government administratively, or that it is always the best vehicle for delivering the services we decide government should provide. But there is ample evidence that the federal government's role over the last years has not been the record of waste, fraud, abuse, and incompetence that is sometimes pictured. The fact is that an interventionist national government has achieved much from which the present advocates of the New Federalism are now benefiting. It has improved the opportunities for tens of millions of Americans to enter the work force in productive, tax-paying jobs. It has improved educational and economic opportunity and social justice in a host of ways. Such opportunities would not have been provided had we relied exclusively on the practices in force before the federal government's activist, interventionist policies began. Of course, to say that in the past much good has been done is not necessarily to defend the status quo. Nor is it to argue that we ought simply to pursue the federal government's intervention as the solution to all problems identified in our political and social debates. At the same time, we must not simply declare or imply, as do the Reagan administration's domestic policies in general and the New Federalism in particular, that there are no domestic national concerns deserving national governmental attention. And if we believe the answer to too much government regulation is to eliminate the regulatory thrust in Washington, then we need only wait to see the regulations spawned in fifty state capitals.

In 1980, when the nation's governors sat down with President Carter before the 1981 budget cycle began, they offered a trade. They said they would accept a 10 percent off-the-top cut in federal aid to state governments in exchange for a significant increase in flexibility and state control over state-administered programs. Former Governor Carter was instinctively responsive to this idea and urged the governors to come back with a more specific proposal concerning where

the 10 percent cut could be made. The 1980 elections inter-
vened before the Carter administration had an opportunity
to see the governors' response. But, in fact, the Reagan administration raised the ante of this deal in 1981—from 10
percent to 25 percent. So the governors, who with enthusiasm embraced the administration's block grant program in
their midwinter meeting in February 1981, found themselves
by spring living with the prospect of a 25 percent reduction in
federal aid in exchange for something called—with considerable uncertainty—"more flexibility."

The Reagan administration's more fully developed 1982
version of the New Federalism offered in the president's
State of the Union address, if enacted, would be the governmental equivalent of the con man's bait-and-switch
routine—made up of one part money and one part power.
The money is a proposed $28 billion trust fund composed of
excise and windfall profit tax revenues. The power is the
promise of state control of over forty programs previously
administered by the federal government.

The switch in this scam is a little more complicated, but a
switch nonetheless. Simply stated, the Reagan proposal
would leave the states in ten years with no money to finance
at least $47 billion worth of services that had been funded by
the federal government. This is the way it would work:

—Congress authorizes a federal takeover of Medicaid for
  which the states will spend approximately $16 billion
  in 1984. A $28 billion trust fund is then established to
  finance forty other programs including health, highways, airports, community development, welfare, food
  stamps, and social services that would be shifted to state
  responsibility.

—Over a ten-year period the trust fund would phase out,
  leaving the states with the "freedom" to tax their residents in order to raise the revenues necessary to continue
  the programs.

An additional wrinkle in all this is that the inevitable in-creases in costs for these services would also have to be financed by state and local taxes. If inflation is kept to a very conservative 5 percent annual average over the next decade, the $28 billion trust fund of 1984 will be worth only $14 billion when the switch is completed. Using this assumption, state governments would have to raise $56 billion in taxes just to keep services at present levels.

Beyond the "now you see it, now you don't" character of the New Federalism, there is mounting evidence that the American people understand and don't like the longer-term consequences of what is being proposed.

A recent national poll conducted for the Democratic party shows that 43 percent of the voters think the Reagan administration will go too far in cutting needed government services that benefit average Americans as well as the poor. The people also understand what the consequences will be if the New Federalism becomes law. Sixty-two percent of the people in the same poll think local property taxes will increase as a result of the president's 1981 program of federal budget and tax cuts. What will they think about a program that leaves the states holding an additional $47 billion of obligations and *no* federal revenues to help pay for them?

In the proposed sorting out of which level of government ought to perform which functions, the Reagan program fails as well. There is no inherent or self-evident logic in the suggested swap of welfare for Medicaid. They are both income-determined programs created to address the national problem of poverty. Why should the states handle one function and the national government the other? Similarly, there is no public finance justification in transferring the burden of government services from a progressive national income tax to regressive excise, property, and sales taxes at the state and local levels. If the president's desire to give state and local government more responsibility is to be realized, why has he not proposed continued federal assistance within a framework of increased authority to the states, counties, and cities?

In short, there is no evidence that the administration has thought all this through in formulating its proposals. The New Federalism seems little more than an expression of the president's personal prejudices against the national government's playing any role in meeting domestic problems, linked to a proposed federal takeover of Medicaid to soften the shift of current federal obligations to the states.

It is not immediately obvious to me, as someone who once served as deputy mayor in a Midwestern city and worked in Illinois state government before coming to Washington, that the property tax in Hennepin County, Minnesota, or Cook County, Illinois, is the best way to pay for the services we agree we want. In other words, the 25 percent cut in 1981 plus the 1982 "bait and switch" will have more fundamental consequences than appear at first glance. Having gained something vaguely termed "increased flexibility" in administration, state and local government will have no choice but to increase taxes while reducing services.

The final—and most important—issue is fairness. In the 1980s it is easy to forget that the original rationale for federal intervention was a realization that certain national needs would have to be addressed with national resources and standards. Majorities of Congress, led by Republican and Democratic presidents, came to this realization because they recognized the disparities not only in tax base but also in service requirements that prevail in different areas of the country. The administration's initiatives will provide a smaller revenue pool with which to meet these requirements, as well as a reliance on more comparatively regressive state and local taxes rather than on the more progressive federal income tax.

It should come as no surprise, therefore, when big-city mayors and urban-county executives prove to be among the most reluctant to accept the intergovernmental agenda of the present administration. These are the elected officials who preside over jurisdictions with the largest dependent populations. It is in big cities and urban counties that the largest number of people will prove to be adversely affected by the policies of the New Federalism.

It is understandable for a governor or any other elected official to want to exercise political responsibility. I am quite sensitive to the pleas of governors and others who have complained with increasing intensity in recent years that they are no more than administrative handmaidens of the federal bureaucracies. Yet the issue of control cannot be decided in a vacuum. Administrative control and flexibility are worthy concerns, but they must be addressed in a broader context. We must ask how these structural changes will affect not only the machinery of government, but the well-being of our citizens.

This president has told the American people that the number one challenge facing our nation is to get government off our backs. We Democrats have a different, more hopeful vision of the capacities of a free people and the American government.

We Democrats do not believe that every problem in America can be solved by government. We know that bureaucracy and red tape are the common enemies of our common public purposes and an unacceptable burden upon our citizens. While strengthening vital protections, the Democratic party has led the way in stripping excess layers of regulation from agencies of government, such as the Occupational Safety and Health Administration, and from whole sectors of our economy, including the banking, trucking, and airline industries.

But from social security to the Voting Rights Act, we Democrats are proud of the contributions we have made through enlightened public policies towards building a more just and prosperous nation. Our task is to make government at all levels a tough, resilient, and lean defender of the public's well-being and the common good.

John McClaughry: "Republicans with a Small 'r' "

President Nixon's "New Federalism" was fundamentally different from that of President Reagan. The centerpiece of Nixon's New Federalism was general revenue sharing, in which the federal government exercises its taxing power to accumulate revenues to send back to the states under supposedly minimum requirements or restrictions.

At the same time, the New Federalism program attempted to convert a number of categorical programs into large-scale block grants. Unfortunately, block grants inevitably turn back into categorical grants. The mandates reappear. The requirements reappear. The earmarking reappears. And this will happen as long as Congress sits in the city of Washington, D.C. Thus the net effect of the Nixon New Federalism has been to bring about what President Andrew Jackson feared when he vetoed the first revenue sharing bill in 1833: that the availability of large grants from the federal government to state and local governments would make state and local officials "the mere instruments and stipendiaries of the central power."

President Reagan has a different view. While he sees block grants as a temporary improvement, he stresses very emphatically that they can be only an interim step. He recognizes that block grants do inevitably turn back into categorical grants over time, thereby eliminating the opportunity to make real reforms. Eugene Eidenberg's view of the federal government as a benevolent entity is somewhat different from my own. My own view is one of a large, shapeless, slimy amoeba slopping and stumbling its way across America, consuming people, property, progress, and paychecks. However, Dr. Eidenberg does raise an important question that very much deserves to be on the agenda—namely, what do Amer-

icans expect government to do for them, and which governments do they expect to do it? Perhaps we have been asking
too much of governments, state and local as well as federal. If
so, then, in our passion for restructuring the responsibilities
among federal, state, and local governments, perhaps we
have lost sight of the proposition that we are asking government to do too much for the people—at least, government as
traditionally considered. Instead, we ought to put new
emphasis not only on transferring functions and tax bases
from Washington to the states—and through them, to the
cities or the counties—but also on finding ways to return
power to the people themselves.

This theme has recurred many times in President
Reagan's pronouncements over the years. For example, in
1975 he followed Jefferson in asking what it was that had
destroyed the rights of man in every government under the
sun. Jefferson and Ronald Reagan answered, "The general-
izing and concentrating of all cares into one body." In his later
years, Jefferson came to believe that the most effective way
for citizens to interact with government was at the ward
level. He saw from colonial Virginia a real capacity of land-
owning citizens at the local level to deal with problems without creating a governmental superstructure that threatened
their independence, stifled their initiative, and eventually
sent them a bill for taxes that was too great to be paid. There
are a lot of theoretical dimensions to that belief, which
Jefferson and Ronald Reagan share. The local community is
the arena of civic action, where citizens perform their duty
as citizens. It is an arena for republican virtue and for democratic participation—republican with a small "r" and democratic with a small "d." In our day, we see a growing movement toward empowering individuals and the neighborhoods, small communities, special districts, and townships.
People are now beginning to demand that the services they
once expected government to deliver be contracted or ar-
ranged for under their immediate control, and largely under
their own taxing base and tax power.

People are thus not merely resorting to the various levels of government, but are going right back to the fundamental question of what government is expected to do for all of us. This is not a call for the wholesale abolition of government down to the neighborhood level. But it does, I think, point to a trend that we would do well in this administration—and the party out of power would do well in its efforts to get back into power—to understand. Where people actually live—not in the halls of Congress and not in the learned academic centers—is where the real questions of federalism for the rest of this century will be decided.

7

DAVID B. SWOAP

Federalism: New Directions at the Department of Health and Human Services

Horizontal and vertical dimensions of federalism. Block grants and the administration's programs. Legislative reforms to welfare programs.

Overall, between 1950 and 1980 federal social spending grew from $20 billion to $300 billion—seven times the rate of inflation. Today the Department of Health and Human Services (HHS) budget is $250 billion, larger than the total budget of any country in the world except the United States and the Soviet Union. The physical size of this department has multiplied correspondingly. As the federal government has given away money, it has also successfully argued in court that it has a right to control how that money is to be spent—creating a cycle of subsidy and control that is largely responsible for the burgeoning bureaucracy.

These dramatic increases in the scope and cost of federal programs have caused the emergence of a new issue in the historic debate over federalism. Today the question is asked: who can best satisfy the "general welfare" clause of the Constitution—local, state, or federal government?

THE ADMINISTRATION'S FEDERALIST POLICY

The congressionally mandated Advisory Commission on Intergovernmental Relations (1980, pp. 45, 87), after a three-year study, warns that the federal government's influence has "become more pervasive, more intrusive, more unmanageable, more ineffective, more costly, and above all, more unaccountable." The very concept of American federalism—the "separation of powers" between federal, state, and local levels of government—is in trouble. The American people are confused about what federalism means, and only a clear restoring of a sense of constitutionalism and constitutional priorities can possibly solve their bewilderment.

This administration's policy was initially directed at reforming existing programs through eliminating waste, fraud, and abuse. Then we turned to the concept of block grants to return authority for programs to the states. Social services can best be handled at the state and local levels because the government unit closest to the people can most efficiently target the truly needy for whom these programs were designed.

Targeting help efficiently depends on the ability to identify and make decisions about varying standards of need in different situations. Many welfare projects experience rapid fluctuations in the people they serve, such as those on Supplemental Security Income (SSI), nursing home residents, and migrant workers. A 1981 General Accounting Office report concluded that families on Aid to Families with Dependent Children (AFDC) receive widely varying benefit packages, and 80 percent of the families in their sample were above the poverty line through a combination of cash and in-kind benefits.* In many cases it is critical, where appropriate, to have a work requirement tied to welfare payments. "Workfare" can be successful only through community involvement—only state and local units can efficiently tailor these programs to meet local goals.

To begin this return of power, there must be increased dialogue between governmental units at all levels. One innovative approach in this direction, developed by Secretary Richard Schweiker of HHS, has been to initiate a "fast-track" system to facilitate review of secretarial discretion requests to modify, remove, or waive certain federal requirements. This system will assure quick responses to governors and their cabinets concerning requests for waivers or deregulation.

Federalism, rightly seen, has not a vertical but rather a horizontal dimension. In a federated republic such as the United States, there is a partnership among the various governmental units, not a hierarchy leading to a single centralized authority. Operationally, the federal government

*It should be noted that, as the GAO report itself indicated, the sample did not contain sufficient statistical validity to enable projections to the AFDC universe.

may well be "first"—but it is "first among equals." Consequently, all levels of government should share in the
decision-making process and in responsibility for implementation; and the Reagan administration has pledged to form
such a partnership in the development of health and human
service programs.

If federalism is viewed horizontally, the federal system will
have the flexibility enabling it to discern more accurately
which areas of government can best serve which purposes.
Thus, the federal government's resources and personnel can
deal best with such matters as conducting research in health
fields, promoting important goals such as disease prevention,
and maintaining agencies such as the Center for Disease
Control, which serves as both a global and a national
resource in the epidemiology of communicable diseases.

By viewing federalism horizontally, it becomes evident
that the management of much of what is termed "welfare"
can best be done on a state and local level. Income patterns
differ not just from state to state, but from locality to locality;
family cohesiveness differs between regions; the role of
family support systems and voluntary organizations is not
the same throughout the nation. All of these variables can
and do affect public assistance and health programs both
quantitatively and qualitatively. For HHS, the administration's changes mean continuing to commit substantial
resources to human needs while slowing the growth in our
spending, in order to move toward a balanced budget so
necessary for economic stability—although the HHS overall
budget in fiscal year (FY) 1982 of $250 billion represents an
increase in outlays of $21.5 billion over 1981. In fact, HHS
received the largest share of the total increase in government spending for FY 1981.

ENDING THE "BIG BROTHER" APPROACH

Many regulations are currently being reviewed that fall within the purview of the Department of Health and Human Services, and we are taking appropriate measures to reduce the number of restrictive regulatory requirements. One of these measures involves studying methods by which HHS can strengthen the role of the department's regional directors. The objective of this formal study is to determine what decision-making authority should rest at the regional level vis-à-vis what authority should remain in Washington; we believe that the best decisions can be made at the regional level by administrators who are most familiar with the problems of the states and localities. In the past, centralized authority has often alienated our state and local counterparts. Moreover, feedback from Washington has sometimes lacked the timeliness and responsiveness necessary to meet local needs. A coordinated regional approach to improve effectiveness is particularly important as we move forward with block grant funding.

Technical assistance is another area that will be redefined by the department so that it no longer is used to measure compliance with federally imposed regulations and guidelines. The "big brother" approach that has been in use is contrary to the theory of federalism and serves only to keep states engulfed in red tape. Our aim is, instead, to move toward the concept of helping states develop their own technology.

Block grants are another key part of the president's domestic program. The *Wall Street Journal* has correctly reported that the block approach is potentially as significant to the federal structure of government as the budget and tax cuts are to the economy. Block grants consolidate federal grant awards once parceled out in a multitude of rigidly defined "categorical" programs, are designed to save con-

siderable overhead costs, and will introduce much-needed
flexibility in program administration. The result will be not
only a more efficient use of funds, but also greater citizen
participation in the control of spending.

The administration initially proposed four block grants to
be administered by our department: Social Services, Health
Services, Preventive Health Services, and Energy and
Emergency Assistance. Under the original block grant legislation, the federal government would make annual grants to
states and territories to support the kinds of services being
consolidated under the blocks. The administration's initial
proposals were characterized by the following features: First,
funds would not be earmarked for specific services. Second,
there would be no maintenance-of-effort requirements nor
any requirements for states to match federal funds. Third,
states would be permitted to transfer up to 10 percent of the
funds from one HHS block to another. Fourth, states would
be required to publish a pre-expenditure report on their program funding intentions and to report publicly on how the
block grant monies were spent, but there would be no requirement for federal approval of these reports or plans.
Finally, states would be required to arrange independent
audits, annually in most cases.

Nearly all aspects of the administration's proposal have
been modified by Congress—the number of blocks, the programs contained therein, and the administrative provisions.
The Omnibus Budget Reconciliation Act of 1981 created
seven health and human service blocks rather than the four
originally proposed. Separate blocks—for Maternal and
Child Health; Alcohol, Drug Abuse, and Mental Health; Primary Care; and Preventive Health Services—have been
developed from the administration's proposed Health Care
and Preventive Health Services blocks. Separate one-
program blocks for Social Services, Community Services Administration, and Low Income and Energy Assistance programs were also proposed by Congress.

Within these seven blocks, there were significant departures from the administration's proposal concerning the package of consolidated programs. The health blocks include nineteen programs, essentially all but three of the major programs proposed by the administration for consolidation. These three—Migrant Health Centers, Venereal Disease Prevention and Treatment, and Family Planning—will remain categorical, although the Primary Care block contains only one program, Community Health Centers.

On the other hand, the Social Services block contains only one program out of the twelve originally proposed by the administration. That block has been pared down to include only programs funded under Title XX of the Social Security Act. All others will remain categorical. The Low Income Energy Assistance block also is a one-program block, although the administration initially proposed to include only two programs in it.

A final area of difference is that the blocks all have more administrative requirements than those proposed by the administration. For example, many contain limitations on administrative costs (which carry with them federal definitions of what constitutes an administrative cost). Some contain matching and maintenance-of-effort requirements. The Maternal and Child Health block requires that a state spend three dollars for every four dollars received from the federal government. The Primary Care block requires states to continue for two years to make grants to community health centers funded by the federal government in FY 1981. Nevertheless, in general, the concept of limited federal rules and oversight has been maintained.

ADVANTAGES OF BLOCK GRANTS

Despite the changes, the final block grant legislation is a significant move toward state responsibility for public services.

The legislation will permit us to show by example that Congress is no wiser and that federal programming is no more effective than state legislatures and state plans.

By functioning less as a taskmaster and more as a resource, the block grant will go a long way toward changing the federal role within the context of federalism. The federal government will become more of an information broker, enabling states to diversify their approaches to providing services. The ultimate goal is to return to the states not only state authority to manage programs that properly belong at the state level, but also to give back the tax sources that will provide their operating revenue. To this end, the president has established and given high priority to the Tax Resources work group to examine the complex issue of returning the appropriate revenue resources. The under secretary of HHS is a member of this work group.

In addition to the block grants, HHS has recommended broad changes in other program areas. Before recent changes in federal law, states were unable to take many steps to make their Medicaid programs more cost-effective. They could not take advantage of economies of scale by buying in bulk and distributing items such as canes or wheelchairs. They could not use competitive bid arrangements to purchase services. They were limited in their ability to contract with cost-efficient health care providers; recipients used higher-cost institutional care because reimbursement was not available for less expensive community services. The department's revisions in program requirements gave the states greater flexibility to design more cost-effective programs as well as to provide for civil penalties against fraud.

Specifically, the reforms will allow states to:

—better determine the scope of their Medicaid programs, given limited resources, and continue to support all essential services for the most needy;

—target optional services to those in need of them;

—adopt new methods of reimbursement to provide for delivery of care at lower costs, such as competitive bidding for medical goods and services and full contracting for services on a prepaid basis; and

—better determine eligibility for benefits.

The department proposed legislative reforms in two of the largest welfare programs—Aid to Families with Dependent Children and Supplemental Security Income (as well as in the Child Support Enforcement Program)—to target benefits more accurately to needy children, the aged, and the disabled. The effects of these changes will be:

—to target those most in need;

—to reduce incentives to remain on public assistance, and to require work;

—to assist the state in collecting unpaid child support payments;

—to improve administration and management of these programs, and to reduce payment errors and fraud.

All too often, states administer programs but program decisions are made at the federal level, tying local administrators' hands and reducing the states to mere administrative districts of the federal government. Worst of all, humanitarian purposes get lost. Many who should be helped are not, while others who need less help are getting a disproportionate share because decisions are made too far away from real needs. Too much stress on federal uniform criteria has caused states to spend inordinate amounts of time and money reporting back to Washington, using scarce program dollars to support the various levels of government and resulting in unnecessary duplication of effort. All this has produced ineffective management that amounts to almost a paralysis of government. Moreover, it must not be forgotten that the private sector has always had a major role in providing public assistance and health programs, which must not be disparaged. Demographically, economically, and politically, government at all levels does and should have its limits.

We believe that the department's proposals respond to the demands of governors, state legislators, and local officials for more flexibility in focusing resources on the needs they know best and in ways best suited to local conditions. The call for such flexibility has been resounding as departmental officials have talked with various national interest groups and elected officials around the country. The message is quite clear: they are urging that the power be given back to its legitimate source, the people.

RESPONSE

Lamar Alexander: "Make Federalism a Part of the Budget"

To make the states stronger, to make them larger partners in American federalism, I have a specific suggestion that the president and his advisors might wish to consider so that his dream of a revitalized federal system is achieved: it is that he make federalism a part of his budget. I have an even more specific suggestion than that: as Governor Babbitt of Arizona and I have proposed, the national government should take over fully the cost and administration of Medicaid, and at the same time the states should fully take over elementary and secondary education and other programs strictly local in character.

What can you do about making states stronger? To start with, you have to realize where you are. Tennessee, for example, is a relatively poor state. But the average Tennessee family's share of the national budget is about $12,000 a year. The average Tennessee family's share of the state budget is only about $2,000 a year. Even a little change in the federal budget makes a big difference in the Tennessee budget. The *increase* in the federal budget last year equaled two-thirds of the total budgets of all the states. That is a very important point to begin with. Now you might say: Well, why didn't the states step in and take up all this initiative over the last forty or fifty years? In that respect, I can agree with everything that Gene Eidenberg said. We don't even need to argue whether or not the goals of the last forty or fifty years were good. The question is, where do we go from here?

You cannot go from a federal system—in which you have for each family a national government that is six times larger in fiscal impact than the state government—suddenly back to a changed situation without thinking very carefully about what you do. So what can you do about it? First, you can remove the rules and regulations. I will give this administration an A+ for trying to remove rules and for even more successfully changing attitudes. The block grant effort was very important to try. It was a significant step, although it only got a little ways. But the attitude of this administration is even more important in terms of just looking for ways within its present authority to make it possible for governors and mayors to exercise more discretion. That is one thing it can do.

There is only one other thing we can do to restore responsibility to state and local governments, and that is to restore their tax base. One way to do that is, simply, every time the national government cuts, state and local governments add back. But that would completely defeat the whole thrust of the president's program. This is what is happening in England today, where violent debates are going on. Nearly every time Mrs. Thatcher reduces the government grant to the local township, the township just automatically raises its taxes. So the whole theory of whether or not reduction of government spending makes any difference in its impact on private economy never gets a chance to be tried because the money is raised at the lower level every time it is cut at the central level. So that is not a part of the plan.

Therefore, the only way that you can restore local tax bases is by looking for specific ways to do it. Block grants ultimately will never work: they eventually become categorical grants again. The only other two ideas that have been suggested are to return revenue sources to state and local governments or to swap. The swap idea is the one that Governor Babbitt and I have suggested.

Both these ideas involve the federal Treasury's losing some money. How much money? Elementary and secondary education, for example, cost the federal government every year less than $6 billion. The state and local governments pay over 90 percent. At the same time, the states pay $15 billion for Medicaid. So a swap of these two programs would cost the federal government $9 billion.

That is why I respectfully suggest that President Reagan and his advisors ought to consider making federalism a part of his budget. For $9 billion more in the federal budget, the national government could accept the program that is most troublesome from the fiscal point of view for every single state: Medicaid. To put Medicaid under a single management is one thing that could make it a less troublesome fiscal problem for everybody. Then let the states, at the same time, concentrate their resources and attention on what ought to be and what is in most cases their primary responsibility: to improve the quality of our rapidly deteriorating system of public education. You can find fifty reasons why that will not work—as you can with any other bold idea. But there are also some very fundamental reasons why such a swap should work.

Mr. Swoap suggested that welfare and similar programs ought to be administered by state and local governments. One wonders what that says about the president's "security net." The president talks about a whole range of programs that have to do with the truly needy. He has apparently accepted and recognized that those programs, properly, are national in character. Taking over welfare doesn't bother me so much if you mean AFDC, although this is not consistent and may even be a little heretical with National Governors' Association policy. We have no problem in Tennessee with keeping its growth under control, because we make most decisions affecting the program. With Medicaid, on the other hand, Washington decides who is eligible, and we have to pay 30 percent of the bill in Nashville. At the same time, we can decide in Nashville what new program to offer, and the national government has to pay 70 percent of the bill. That is no way to do anything. No wonder the program is out of control.

With regard to transferring the responsibility, we have only about three dozen employees in Tennessee administering the Medicaid program. Most of the program is contracted out to an organization like Blue Cross for general administration. I think of Medicaid, not in terms of welfare, but in terms of its relationship to Medicare. Medicare is already a $55 billion program, which is three times as large as the federal expenditure on Medicaid. As Governor Busbee has often pointed out, there is no way that you can control health care costs unless you work on both programs at once. I would think you could do that more effectively at the national level. In our state, Medicaid has grown from a $30 million program to a $500 million program today.

People have a real fear that Medicaid will cost more if the federal government takes it over. I think that this has been proved wrong already. What other program has grown from $30 million to $500 million in one state—a state with a very moderate program? I think Medicaid would have grown less if *either* the state or the federal government had run it exclusively. Obviously, the state cannot run it with a block grant because the federal government would never grant the full authority necessary to do it. Moreover, the state probably does not have the resources to do it.

So here is a specific suggestion in response to the ideas offered by the administration. It boils down to the idea that the national government, properly, could concern itself with those programs that have to do with redistributing the national wealth and taking care of those who need help. That accounts for at least 10 percent of the gross national product. The national defense is another 5 percent. Pay off the debt and that's about it. There are a few other things that the national government is involved in, but that is about it. The great number of other federal activities comprise only a relatively small part of the cost.

I think that governors are eager—many Democrats and many Republicans—to take on the hard responsibilities of being accountable. And we believe most of our constituents would like to know whom to blame, who is to be held accountable for what happens or what doesn't happen. One way to do it, in the Medicaid program, is to say, "Call your congressman." One way to do it, if Johnny can't read, is to make it clear that no one in Washington can teach him how. And if you do that in the context of everything else that is happening right now it will relieve a great deal of fiscal pressure on state and local governments.

So, in summary, my hope is that the president will consider making federalism a part of his next budget. Otherwise that most important part of his dream stands the best chance of getting shattered along the way.

IV

Revenue Reallocation
in the Federal System

8

WM. CRAIG STUBBLEBINE

Revenue Reallocation in the Federal System: Options and Prospects

Redirecting federal funding. Block grants, matching grants-in-aid. Reversing the incentive skew. Competition in interfiscal jurisdictions. Freedom of choice.

Debates over public policy are in part exercises in prediction. At the core of the administration's "New Federalism" proposals are changes in taxing and spending arrangements. To evaluate these changes, one must understand their probable effects not simply on public spending but also on the incentives built into the political process. How will state and local governments respond to changes in federal funding? More specifically, how will they accommodate both to decreases in total funding and to a redirection of funds away from specific programs?

It is impossible at this point to present the empirical results that would illuminate these issues; and space does not allow a review of how this nation came to its current situation.[1] What can be done is to develop a theoretical framework within which a more comprehensive study might proceed.

I

The probable responses of state and local governments to a redirection of federal funding can be illuminated, at least in part, by starting with a simplified case. Assume that two units of government, a federal government and a state (or local) government, each exercise responsibility over a given geographic area. A proposal is made to shift the funding of some government program from the state level to the federal level. That is, state taxes will be decreased and federal taxes increased. If the federal government uses exactly the tax system that has been utilized at the state level, nothing will have changed. The constraints on every individual or household in the geographic area will remain unchanged: the tax cost borne by each voter for each increment of the government spending program will be the same whether funded at the federal or state (or local) level. Voter propensity or desire to fund government services also will be unchanged. In consequence, the level of public services and private services will remain unaffected by this shift. Since no one gains and no one loses, there also will be little if any enthusiasm either to press for or to oppose such a shift.

The world rarely is so simple. The federal government encompasses many states, which in turn encompass many localities. For the sake of simplicity, focus hypothetically on just two local communities. Unless the socioeconomic characteristics of the two communities are identical (and thus also identical to the nation as a whole), a shift in funding responsibility will offer the possibility of altering the constraints faced by households in each of the local communities.

To illustrate, assume that both the local and federal levels of government employ a proportional tax on incomes and that the households in one community have incomes twice those in the other. A dollar of government spending financed locally will have the same tax price in each community. Those same dollars funded at the federal level will mean a higher tax price for the residents of the higher-income community and a lower tax price for the residents of the lower-income community.[2]

Two implications flow from this setting. First, voters from the higher-income community will tend to oppose—and voters from the lower-income community will tend to favor—a shift in funding responsibility from the local community to the federal level. Second, voters from the higher-income community will seek to reduce—and voters from the lower-income community will seek to increase—the amount of federal government spending relative to the amounts each would seek when funded locally. The exception to this would be a federal grants-in-aid program that returned to each local community an amount equal to the taxes paid by the residents of that community. Federal programs rarely, if ever, are so structured.

Separately, different levels of government typically employ different tax structures. If the federal government employs a progressive tax on income while local or state governments employ essentially proportional income taxes, a shift in funding from the state or local level to the federal level will increase the tax prices faced by upper-income families and decrease the tax prices faced by lower-income families. As with differing socioeconomic characteristics, the same two implications flow from this setting.

In combination, differing socioeconomic characteristics and differing tax structures enhance the tax price differentials among levels of government and the implications for fiscal federalism. Voters from higher-income communities will tend to oppose a shift in funding responsibility to the federal level and, if it is shifted, to seek a reduction in the amount of federal funding relative to the amount that otherwise would have been funded locally. Voters from lower-income communities will tend to favor a shift in funding responsibility to the federal level and, if it is shifted, to seek an increase in the amount of federal funding relative to the amount that otherwise would have been funded locally.

This simple "pencil exercise" illustrates the tax price characteristics of funding government activities at various levels of government. Still more insight into the character of intergovernmental relations may be had by amending the setting to incorporate various grants-in-aid from the more inclusive federal to the less inclusive state or local governments.

The first and most obvious grant-in-aid formula is one in which federal funds are distributed to local communities proportional to their population. For a fixed sum generated by federal taxation, the tax price characteristics are the same as those examined above. Higher-income communities will face higher tax prices, and lower-income communities will face lower tax prices, for the federal portion of the funding of some government good or service. Local communities will face more or less equal tax prices for the additional funding done locally. The grant has a "wealth" effect on localities, decreasing available resources in upper-income communities and increasing resources available in lower-income communities while leaving unchanged the trade-off between private and public spending at the local level.

The tax price differentials will be widened further if the grant-in-aid is distributed in a way inversely proportional to community income. If lower-income communities receive proportionately more federal funding than upper-income communities, lower-income communities will have greater incentives to favor shifting funding to the federal level. As with the per capita distribution formula, receipt of the grant will have wealth effects but no local relative price effects. On balance, higher-income communities will enjoy less—and lower-income communities more—of *both* private and public consumption than they would in the absence of the grant.

If local communities have been funding government goods and services locally, introduction of a federal grant-in-aid will induce some substitution of private spending for local taxation. The additional taxes being paid to—in combination with the additional resources being received from—the more inclusive government will displace the previous local equilibrium between private and public consumption. If grant spending simply is added to local government spending, residents of all communities will come to perceive that too much is being spent by their local government. In response, local taxes will tend to decline, though typically by less than the grant received, and spending on privately marketed goods and services will increase. Local "fiscal effort," measured by the ratio of local taxes to local income, will decline in all local communities—even as total government taxing and spending increases.

By contrast with "block" grant formulae, matching grants-in-aid have both wealth and relative price effects on local communities. The wealth effects are analogous to those of block grants, in the sense that funding at the more inclusive federal level of government has the potential to redistribute resources among local communities. The obvious change in relative prices follows from the "matching" aspect, with the local community funding only a portion of each dollar spent on the government activity in question.

Matching grants also carry the potential to disturb the equality between (marginal) tax price and (average) tax cost. While recognizing implicitly that the local community's residents will be responsible for some portion of the total federal funding, residents also may reason that the burden of financing the grant received by *their* community will be shared by all residents of the more inclusive federal government. The federal portion of their tax price may be perceived as approaching zero. In consequence, all localities may press for an increase in matching funds, even those communities for which the average tax cost exceeds the costs of pure local funding.

As with block grants, matching grants will induce some substitution of private spending for local taxation. The additional taxes and resources implicit in the match by the more inclusive federal government will displace the previous local equilibrium between private and public consumption. There will be less in the way of local taxes and more private spending on goods and services. Local "fiscal effort" will decline, even as total government taxing and spending increases.

What about the difference between "block" grants and "matching" grants-in-aid? Under matching grants, there is a perceived decline in the tax price of government-supplied goods and services relative to the price of private goods. This will tend to induce communities to spend more publicly under matching grants than under block grants. That is, the relative price effects of matching grants will reinforce the wealth effects. In the final analysis, communities may be largely indifferent between comparable block grants and matching grants, but spending by all levels of government will tend to be higher under matching grants.

It should be noted that the implications of grants-in-aid apply to whole communities, as units. A lower-income household in an upper-income community will have as much incentive to oppose introduction of grants-in-aid as will an upper-income household in that community. Similarly, an upper-income household in a lower-income community will have as much incentive to favor introduction of grants as will a lower-income household in that community.

II

The political economy of fiscal federalism is more complex than the simple characteristics touched upon so far. Congress has tended to place conditions on grants-in-aid to state and local governments, and these restrictions complicate the impact of the grants. Several hundred grant programs are now being federally funded, with a variety of formulae to determine the amounts received by any given fiscal jurisdiction. There are several motives for this.

The first simply may be a sense of fiscal trusteeship. Having levied the taxes, Congress feels a responsibility to ensure that the funds are "well spent." If a grant is justified on the basis of stimulating local consumption of some specific good or service for the benefit of nonresidents, accountability demands that the community in fact expand total spending on that good. Such would be the case, for example, if federal highway funds were designed to promote better highways for those traveling through—rather than to—a community.

If the grant is justified on the basis that a community is "too poor" to maintain an adequate level of public services for its citizens, accountability may seem to demand that the community not simply substitute federal funding for local funding of community services. Inclusion of a "fiscal effort" component seeks to bias the trade-off between private and public spending in favor of public spending. This affects tax prices in much the same way as does a matching grant.

In this connection, it should be noted that the very notion of "poorness" brings with it a built-in incentive for expansion of grants-in-aid programs. Communities fall along a continuum from the very poor to the very wealthy. A program that initially singles out the very poor leaves the next most poor without federal support. These communities, in turn, plead that they look much more like those receiving federal support than the average community that does not. Con-

gress responds, therefore, by raising the dividing line between "poor" recipients and nonrecipients. Having done so, it
leaves the next level of communities to plead their own relative "poverty."

Congress also may be motivated by a response to the local
special interests that have been vocal in seeking federal
funding in the first instance. Left to its own devices, even
with its munificent fiscal capacity, a community may be nig-
gardly in funding some good or service of interest to some
subset of the community's body politic. These interests then
seek government funding in response to tax price incentives; shifting the focus of fiscal responsibility to the federal
government merely provides greater tax price leverage. In
the extreme, federal funding with tax prices perceived to approach zero may be critical to achieving any local enthusiasm for shifting responsibility for the good or service in question from the private sector to the public sector. Conditioning
the grant as to specific use seeks to ensure that the community in fact responds to this segment of its population.

A third motive may involve local government officials who,
independently of the body politic, determine that the community "should" spend more in certain areas. An element of
duplicity may enter here. In the local legislature, the official
deplores the federal restrictions that prevent utilizing
federal funds more productively from the standpoint of the
local electorate. Before Congress, the same official might
promote—explicitly or implicitly—the imposition of such
restrictions as a way of sidestepping the desires of those who
elect or appoint him to office.

III

The enthusiasm for "revitalizing" American fiscal federalism has come from voter realization that, in yielding to the

tax price incentives to shift fiscal responsibility to the federal level, people have ended up receiving less for more. This proposition will be contested bitterly in the months to come by those who perceive that their interests will be less favorably served if responsibility is relocated to state and local levels.

This skewing of incentives is reversible. Categorical block grants restrict the ability of Congress to impose conditions on grants. This will surely lead to local budgeting more in keeping with the interests of the broader body politic. Elimination or weakening of these federal mandates will shift public spending away from those goods and services sought by special interest groups toward those sought by majorities of the local electorates. It will eliminate the bias in favor of public as opposed to private spending, and consequently will lead to generally lower levels of public services in state and local fiscal jurisdictions.

Reducing the volume of federal grant funding will reduce the redistribution of resources among communities associated with those grants. The reduction of redistribution will tend to increase the volume of public services in upper-income communities and to reduce the volume in lower-income communities, while increasing local fiscal effort in both. The direction of change will be independent of whether or not federal tax reduction accompanies, and is more or less equal to, the reduction in the volume of federal grants. That is, local taxes will tend to rise, though generally by less than the grants withdrawn.

If the direction of change occasioned by a reduction in the volume of federal grants is clear, the magnitudes of the shifts will be dependent upon accompanying factors. Congress has enacted a significant reduction in personal and corporate income taxes for the coming years. The consequence will be to release to the states more taxing capacity than would be available if federal taxes had not been reduced. However, reductions in these federal taxes do nothing to change the tax price considerations that have controlled state and local spending at the relevant margins of choice. The same implications would attend proposals to reduce federal excise taxes.

These federal tax reductions *may* signal the states to levy additional taxes in response to what may be called an "announcement effect." However, in an era of voter disinclination to support additional taxes, this would seem an unlikely outcome. Voters have spoken out constantly and eloquently against higher taxes at every level of government.

Moreover, federal taxation differs significantly from state taxation in at least one important respect. When taxes are levied locally rather than federally, households have incentives to shift their private activities—whether place of residence or job location or point of consumption purchase—in response to local tax rate differentials. The greater the differential, the greater the incentive. This interfiscal jurisdiction competition tends to restrain localities in their taxing decisions more severely than it does the federal government.[3] That households have become acclimated to a federal tax does not preclude jurisdictions' sensing an opportunity to compete for tax revenues and tax base as a federal tax is reduced or eliminated.

The major effect of federal grant reductions, therefore, will tend to be a general decline in the share of state personal income going to state and local government spending, *inclusive* of federal grants. In the process of shifting fiscal responsibility to less inclusive governments, the biggest declines will be in those communities that benefited most from federal grants. Relatively low-income states will benefit least from the wealth effects of federal tax reductions. Across-the-board cuts in federal grants, therefore, are likely to impact most heavily on lower-income communities in lower-income states. Congress can soften this impact by differentially reducing grants to higher-income states and, within states, to higher-income communities. Progressively increasing the importance of fiscal capacity in grant distribution formulae during the period over which federal grants are phased out will reverse the process by which these grants first became available to all or most communities, rich or poor.

It is important to note that most federal taxes have their counterparts at the level of state government, not local government—personal income, corporate income, and various excise taxes. Reducing federal taxes will not translate directly into additional local tax base. Whether it translates into local revenues will depend upon the response of state legislatures—first, in replacement with state levies, and second, in the states' funding their own grants-in-aid programs for the benefit of local communities.

IV

The first law of economics is that a thing is neither good nor bad save the alternatives make it so. The choice facing the American people today is whether to continue the process of shifting fiscal responsibility to the federal government, a process that has been accelerating since the mid-1960s, or whether to reverse that process. At the heart of this choice are two major issues.

The first is raised in the notion of *federal* government versus *central* government. This nation was founded on a concept of independent units of government making their own decisions and living with the consequences of those decisions. Both independence and responsibility have been eroded by the continuing shift of fiscal responsibility from less-inclusive to more-inclusive units of government.

If Congress and the American people are to proceed constructively, they must learn to appreciate the distinction between "federal programs" and programs addressing "commonly shared concerns." National defense is the epitome of a federal program: federal coordination is crucial to its success, and federal financing is both required and appropriate.

But there are many commonly shared concerns in society that do not require programs of national scope. Truancy is an example. Every school district in the nation has had and will have students who would rather play than study. The success or failure of any given school district in dealing with its truancy will have little or no impact on the prospects for success or failure in any other school district. A federal truancy grant would affect only the distribution of the tax burden, not the level of truancy. That there is a commonly shared concern does not imply the need for a federal program, however responsive the concern may be to the inherent tax price incentives. Yet for the most part, the expansion in federal grant funding over the last two decades has been addressed to just such concerns.

Second, there is the problem of balancing freedom of individual choice against equality of consumption. There is at least the suggestion in congressional grant formulae that more government spending is preferable to more private spending and that public spending should be more nearly equal among communities. The grant programs that have emerged over the years clearly have promoted a significant redistribution of resources and consumption among communities as well as among individuals. In the eyes of some, this has not gone far enough, but most voters now appear supportive of efforts to reverse direction, at least in part.

States differ in their relative per capita incomes and, therefore, in their relative *willingness* to fund government goods and services. The plea that the states have their own fiscal problems largely translates into an observation that their electorates are unwilling to fund programs from their own tax sources. Federal grants may have meant added benefits to some special interest groups, but this does not imply necessarily that withdrawal of these grants faces states and localities with *new* fiscal responsibilities. Students of public finance have not been particularly sensitive to the distinction between the tax price incentives that have resulted in the shifting of fiscal responsibility and the income redistributive aspects of these shifts. Even if income distribution is argued to be a proper federal concern, yielding to tax price incentives in a fiscal federalism is not.

Current discussions typically raise either or both of two questions: "Can state and local governments assume the additional fiscal responsibilities implied by administration proposals to revitalize American fiscal federalism?" and "Will they?" To the first, the answer is an emphatic, "Yes, they can." To the second, the answer is, "Yes, they will—but only in part."

RESPONSE

Benjamin L. Cardin: "Perspective from State Government"

I want to respond to some of Craig Stubblebine's comments from a special perspective—as a state official who is now faced with the new role that federalism is putting upon state officials.

I represent Baltimore City in the Maryland legislature. Baltimore City depends, to a great extent, on federal programs. Despite this fact, I was a strong supporter of the president's initiative to redress the imbalance of federalism and return to state governments those activities best suited for state government along with the revenue sources to carry out that new level of responsibility.

I supported the president because I honestly believed—and still believe—that in light of the new budgetary stringency it is more important than ever for all levels of government to use public dollars as efficiently as possible, and that we can have more accountability at the state and local levels than at the federal level because we are closer to the people. So it will ultimately be in Baltimore City's best interests to have a more efficient, effective system of delivering public goods.

However, there are some problems. According to our legislature's fiscal experts, under the federal government's proposals we would receive in this budget year approximately $192 million less in federal aid. The president's proposals would also cause us to lose another $83 million of aid to our

153

subdivisions. In addition, the federal tax cuts will reduce tax receipts in the state of Maryland since, along with many other states, Maryland long ago tied its own tax schedule to the federal tax rate in order to reduce taxpayer confusion.

Those of us in state government have real problems. We were told that we would receive the fiscal ability to carry out this new role in federalism. Instead, we find out that our fiscal capability is going to be significantly less than it was a year ago. That is why it is so important to stress that we must turn our attention to the fiscal capabilities of state and local governments. There are several considerations.

First, revenue sources must be commensurate with the new responsibilities.

Second, there must be a growth in these revenues. There has been a lot of discussion about transferring the gasoline tax back to state government, presumably with a reduced federal role in the transportation program. However, costs of transportation programs are going up at 16, 18, and 20 percent a year—and gasoline tax receipts cannot possibly go up rapidly enough to match these costs. The same is true of many other taxes under discussion concerning their return to state government.

Then there is the problem of determining a fair distribution among the states. The income capacity of the different states varies widely—from Maine, at 66 percent of the national norm, to Connecticut, which has 134 percent of the national norm. These differences must be addressed by the federal government in returning revenues to state government. What really worries us at the state level is the idea that states could increase their fiscal capability by raising taxes. This idea ignores political reality. If we at state government want to support the president's initiative to reduce taxes and reduce government spending, we cannot turn around and increase our taxes—when the president is indicating that the thrust of his whole economic policy is based upon the reduction of federal taxes. The idea is politically impossible.

So what are the choices? What are we looking for? We need discussions about the revenues that are to be made available to state government. General revenue sharing is a real possibility. However, we start to get concerned when we hear that we have already taken care of that in the discussions of categorical versus block grants. Theoretically, the consolidation of categorical grants into block grants should allow us to perform greater levels of service for fewer dollars. But we cannot make up the 20 percent funding cut to the State of Maryland this year. Block grants do not give us the extra fiscal capability to carry on the new responsibilities that the federal government is suggesting should rest with the states.

There should be discussion about general revenue sharing to the states, federal tax credits for income tax, or a sales tax at the state level.

Every state in this nation is going to be in a much more difficult fiscal position this coming year as a result of the president's and Congress's initiatives in federalism. What concerns us the most has been the absence of discussion about revenue turn-backs. We do agree with the initiative on federalism, but that initiative must take careful account of the fiscal capabilities of local governments.

9

ALBERT J. DAVIS*

Fiscal Effects
of New Federalism

New Federalism proposals—Reagan, Durenberger, the NGA. The "swap" component: food stamps, AFDC, and Medicaid. Variations between state responses. Protecting state and local governments.

Considerable public discussion of the "New Federalism" has focused on broad, thematic concerns that tap strong currents of public feeling. How responsible should government be held for the well-being of individual citizens? Which level of government is most "responsive" to citizen needs? What is

*This chapter summarizes the work of the taxation and finance staff of the Advisory Commission on Intergovernmental Relations (ACIR). These views are those of the author and do not necessarily represent those of ACIR members.

the value of decentralized versus centralized political power? These are questions that arouse powerful emotions on both sides. Yet the workability of any New Federalism proposal must finally be decided not only on the basis of general themes, but also on the merits of the specific details by which the proposal will achieve its goals. Public opinion polls in recent years have registered a generally high level of confidence in state and local government. There seems to be strong support among the American people for some devolution of power to states and localities. But it is difficult to resolve exactly how that devolution is to be accomplished.

Over recent months the staff of the federal Advisory Commission on Intergovernmental Relations has undertaken a number of studies exploring the probable effects of various federalist schemes. What follows is a comparison of the projected impact resulting from each of three current New Federalism proposals: (1) the administration's original initiative, (2) the proposal of Senator David Durenberger (R–Minnesota), and (3) the plan of the National Governors' Association (NGA). The main features of the three proposals are summarized in table 1.

THE FISCAL BALANCE ISSUE

One key question is whether the amount of revenue turned back to the states will suffice to cover the new responsibilities that they will assume. To put the same question more technically, will any or all of the New Federalism proposals put forward in recent months achieve "aggregate fiscal balance"?

Whether a fiscal balance or "match" can be achieved by each of the three proposals depends on the dollar amounts associated with each relevant program and resource component. It is necessary to project the costs that will be assumed by the states when they take over responsibility for income security or other programs as well as the revenues that would be newly available to them. The projection of costs and revenues depends on assumptions regarding future economic conditions, demographic changes, and legislative and budget decisions.

Two sets of budget assumptions are used here to simulate the fiscal effects of the three New Federalism designs.

The first set of simulations (Case I) is based on projections consistent with the administration's budget, while the second set (Case II) uses projections prepared by the Congressional Budget Office (CBO) for key program and resource components.[1] Also, in Case I we assume that the cost to the states of picking up responsibility for the terminated grant programs is the same in nominal dollars throughout the period 1984–1991. In Case II, the cost of these programs is assumed to increase at 3 percent per year, an amount less than inflation projected for that period.

Since the designers of all three New Federalism proposals intended to achieve aggregate fiscal balance, and since the building blocks allow some flexibility, we have adjusted trust fund amounts as needed in each simulation to show a beginning fiscal balance in 1984. In succeeding years, imbalances develop because each of the various program and resource components has its own growth dynamics. The results of our simulations are summarized in table 2.

Findings

Through 1987 all three New Federalism proposals protect the states as a collectivity from any losses. Under the president's budget assumptions, the surplus to the states ranges from $4.9 billion in 1987 in the administration's plan to $11.3 billion in the Durenberger plan. The alternative budget assumption suggests smaller surpluses ranging from $500 million under the administration's plan to $4.6 billion under the NGA plan.

Table 1
Overview of Alternative New Federalism Plans

	Administration	Durenberger	NGA
Governmental roles			
Medicaid	Federalize	Federalize	Federalize
Food stamps	Turn back	Turn back[1]	Retain as federal[2]
AFDC	Turn back	Turn back[1]	Retain as grant[2]
Other	Turn back 60 to 70 grants[3]	Turn back 60 to 70 grants[3]	Turn back 50 to 60 grants[3] (transportation excluded)
Resource return for states[4]			
Transition period	Trust fund	Trust fund	Trust fund
Dollar amount	$28b	$28b	$13b[5]
Full protection	1984–1987	1984	1984
Partial protection	1988–1991: excise phase-out occurs	1985–1988: part by formula	1985–1988: part by formula
Growth	No	Yes	No
Post-transition period			
Amount and method	$11b via excise repeal	$11b excise return, plus permanent trust fund to grow ($33b to $36b in 1988)	Subject to later determination
Federal-state balance as of 1988[6]	For the states, a loss more likely than a gain[7]	Gain for the states	Gain for the states
Distribution	By excise tax bases	Partly by excise bases, trust fund amounts by grant formula sensitive to fiscal capacity	Subject to later determination

Assurances for Medicaid or public assistance beneficiaries	No need for public assistance provisions; no Medicaid provisions	Same as Reagan plus mandate that state assure minimum resources/services for families by type; no Medicaid provisions	Maintenance of effort 1984–1987 for states for public assistance; no Medicaid provisions
Assurances for local governments, other former grantees	1984: former grants to be funded by the state at previous level (all grantees); 1985–1987 phaseout.	Same as Reagan for 1984–1987, then 1988–1998 phaseout. No provision for other former grantees	Two-part pass-through requirement 1984–1987: 100% for former direct federal-local grants; 15% for former non-ed. federal-state grants. No provision for other former grantees

[1] The senator's plan reflected the idea that, while states would run public assistance programs with considerable discretion, the federal government would still have a financing role and would discharge it via the trust fund grants that are part of his plan.

[2] The NGA, strictly speaking, suggested that disposition of public assistance responsibilities be an issue that is deferred for further negotiations.

[3] Counted as of FY 1982.

[4] States would also obtain fiscal relief via federalization of Medicaid. Distribution of this relief depends both on amounts states would have spent on Medicaid and changes in federal spending on Medicaid.

[5] For 1984–1988, under the NGA plan, the trust fund would be smaller ($13b versus $28b), since there are no AFDC or food stamp burdens to be placed on the states.

[6] Neither the phaseout of the oil windfall profits tax nor reduced federal budgets implying lower federal taxes are counted toward achieving aggregate fiscal balance.

[7] Beyond 1988, a gain for the states becomes possible, assuming that Medicaid costs lifted from the states would show greater growth than the cost of meeting responsibilities turned back.

Table 2
Gains (+) and Losses (−) for the States from Three New Federalism Proposals under Alternative Budget Projections,* 1984–1991
($ billion)

Proposal	Budget assumptions	1984	1985	1986	1987	1988	1989	1990	1991
Administration	Case I	$0.0	$1.4	$3.2	$ 4.9	$ 2.3	−$ 0.3	−$ 2.6	−$ 4.3
	Case II	0.0	0.5	0.4	0.5	− 4.5	− 9.1	− 11.6	− 17.6
Durenberger	Case I	0.0	3.2	7.0	11.3	15.8	20.8	26.0	32.3
	Case II	0.0	0.5	0.4	0.7	2.9	5.8	8.8	12.3
NGA	Case I	0.0	1.7	3.8	6.0	8.3	[To be determined]		
	Case II	0.0	1.9	3.1	4.6	6.5			

*Assumptions:

Case I

(1) Cost of AFDC, food stamps, and state savings from Medicaid based on administration budget projection.

(2) Cost of turned-back grant programs assumed to remain constant in nominal dollars from 1984 on.

Case II

(1) Cost of AFDC, food stamps, and state savings from Medicaid based on CBO projection.

(2) Cost of turned-back grant programs assumed to increase 3 percent per annum.

All projections past 1987 calculated by Advisory Commission on Intergovernmental Relations using growth rates, implicit in the administration and Congressional Budget Office forecasts, for the prior period.

After 1987 the simulations reveal a divergence of fiscal outcomes: the Durenberger and NGA proposals show surpluses, while the administration's proposal shows shortfalls for the states as a group.[2] Even if the administration's budget assumptions for Aid to Families with Dependent Children (AFDC), food stamps, and Medicaid prove correct, the administration's proposal would result in a small shortfall starting in 1989 and lasting through 1992. A shortfall of this magnitude, however, could easily be averted by arranging for a slower phasedown of the trust fund. If the alternative set of budget assumptions is the basis of the simulation, the prognosis for the states is bleaker. The shortfalls would be significantly larger ($17.6 billion in 1991) and would last longer.

The Durenberger and NGA plans produce surpluses for the states in 1987 and all future years. For example, using the president's budget assumptions, a simulation of the Durenberger plan shows that it could be costly from a federal point of view, producing a state surplus of $32.3 billion in 1991.

The substantial variations in fiscal outcomes stem from the design of the programs involved. AFDC, food stamps, and, to a lesser extent, Medicaid, are responsible for much of the variation and hence uncertainty in predicting the fiscal implications of the various New Federalism programs. Under current law, all of these programs are "entitlements"; spending levels consequently depend on economic conditions and rates of utilization. The projection of future costs varies, reflecting both different forecasts of economic performance and different assumptions about congressional reaction to the administration's proposals to reshape the affected programs.

THE PUBLIC ASSISTANCE ISSUE

The "swap" component of the president's federalism initiative would reorganize federal and state/local responsibilities in two major areas—medical care for the disadvantaged and income maintenance—by restructuring three major programs: food stamps, Aid to Families with Dependent Children, and Medicaid. Currently, the food stamp program is fully funded by the federal government; AFDC and Medicaid are jointly financed by the state and federal governments. The administration's proposal would completely federalize the Medicaid program and, as a *quid pro quo,* the states would take over full financial responsibility for food stamps and AFDC. Senator Durenberger has said he is willing to go along with President Reagan's welfare turn-back, provided there is fiscal protection for the states and federal standards are established for state welfare programs. However, the NGA initially rejected the welfare turn-back; the governors have long argued for full federal financing of all welfare.

Any swap of welfare programs between levels of government raises two sets of issues: one broadly philosophical, and another empirical. The broader issue is what level of government should be responsible for the poor. The empirical issues concern what level of assistance states would actually end up providing through wholly state-financed welfare systems, and what changes might occur in Medicaid benefits as a result of federalization. What concerns us here are primarily the empirical issues.

There is great variation among states today in levels of AFDC and Medicaid benefits. Full state control over public assistance would thus seem to lead to continued diversity in benefits, or perhaps even to an increase in variation. Moreover, variation could grow substantially as states take over the now uniform food stamp program. To the extent that current disparities in benefits are related to state ability to finance these benefits, a program to boost the fiscal capacity of the poorer states through new federal grants would help prevent benefits from becoming more variable under full state responsibility.

Some variation in benefits may, however, be desirable. States have different living costs and differences in benefits available under other human services programs. There are also valid differences of opinion over the point at which benefits create excessive dependency among recipients or overburden a state's taxpayers. Moreover, variations in benefits can produce uniformity in a *relative* sense—that is, in comparison to an area's own reference point for an adequate income. For example, the sum of the maximum AFDC and food stamp benefits per person in Mississippi is 51 percent of the average Mississippian's personal income. In the District of Columbia, where the maximum AFDC benefit per person is almost three times as high, the sum of maximum AFDC and food stamps is only 44 percent of average income.

Uniformity of benefits does not imply uniform participation rates among the states. For example, uniform food stamp eligibility standards result in participation by 21 percent of Mississippi's population but only 3 percent of Wyoming's. High participation rates within an area may, it has been argued, undermine both public support for the program and its effectiveness in reducing dependency. Thus, the data in table 3 on state-by-state patterns in Medicaid and public assistance do not by themselves indicate at what point variations in benefit levels among the states can be considered excessive. From this perspective, if federal benefit standards are to accompany a turn-back program, these standards should be formulated with some regard for the variation in conditions among the states.

The second issue involves the federalization of Medicaid. The standard set by a particular federal program can have significant implications for the states. If a new Medicaid pro-

Table 3
State Fiscal Capacity, Poverty Levels, and Assistance Levels or Spending, 1980

States	ACIR fiscal capacity index	Persons in poverty as % of population	Medicaid outlays per recipient	Maximum* monthly AFDC grant	Combined maximum* AFDC/food stamps		
					Yearly	As % of 1980 poverty threshold	As % of state per capita income
Alabama	76	17.9%	$ 813	$118	$3,612	55%	48%
Alaska	260	10.1	1,571	514	8,952	109	64
Arizona	89	12.4	0	202	4,608	70	52
Arkansas	79	18.7	1,057	161	4,128	63	57
California	117	11.3	798	463	6,804	104	62
Colorado	113	10.2	1,280	311	5,427	83	54
Connecticut	112	8.7	1,612	406	6,324	96	54
Delaware	111	11.9	924	266	5,148	78	50
District of Columbia	111	18.9	1,327	286	5,316	81	44
Florida	100	13.0	782	195	4,536	69	50
Georgia	82	16.4	1,075	164	4,164	63	52
Hawaii	107	10.0	899	468	7,956	105	79
Idaho	88	12.7	1,182	282	5,280	80	66
Illinois	108	11.5	1,136	302	5,448	83	52
Indiana	92	9.8	1,728	255	5,064	77	57
Iowa	105	9.4	1,293	360	4,940	90	53

Kansas	109	10.2	1,352	345	5,820	64	58
Kentucky	83	18.4	721	188	4,452	68	59
Louisiana	109	18.9	1,138	173	4,272	65	51
Maine	80	12.9	787	280	5,268	80	67
Maryland	99	9.9	1,021	270	5,184	79	50
Massachusetts	96	9.8	1,288	379	6,096	93	60
Michigan	97	11.1	1,101	462	6,828	104	69
Minnesota	102	9.3	1,817	417	6,420	98	66
Mississippi	69	24.5	687	96	3,348	51	51
Missouri	94	12.4	919	248	5,004	76	56
Montana	113	12.4	1,354	259	5,088	77	60
Nebraska	97	10.4	1,532	335	5,736	87	61
Nevada	155	8.5	1,782	262	5,112	78	48
New Hampshire	97	8.7	1,603	346	5,820	89	64
New Jersey	105	9.7	1,118	360	5,940	90	54
New Mexico	107	17.4	800	220	4,764	73	61
New York	90	13.4	1,985	477	6,924	105	68
(New York City)	navl	navl	navl	(394)	(6,228)	(95)	(61)
North Carolina	80	14.6	1,065	192	4,500	68	58
North Dakota	108	12.8	1,488	334	5,724	87	65
Ohio	97	10.5	1,001	263	5,124	78	54
Oklahoma	117	13.3	1,046	282	5,280	80	58
Oregon	103	11.3	646	339	6,264	95	67

(table continued on next page)

Table 3 (continued from previous page)

State Fiscal Capacity, Poverty Levels, and Assistance Levels or Spending, 1980

States	ACIR fiscal capacity index	Persons in poverty as % of population	Medicaid outlays per recipient	Maximum* monthly AFDC grant	Combined maximum* AFDC/food stamps Yearly	As % of 1980 poverty threshold	As % of state per capita income
Pennsylvania	93	10.5%	$ 846	$318	$5,592	85%	59%
Rhode Island	84	10.3	1,255	453	6,224	95	66
South Carolina	75	15.9	768	129	3,744	57	52
South Dakota	90	16.1	1,575	321	5,616	85	72
Tennessee	79	17.0	1,071	122	3,660	56	47
Texas	124	14.8	1,426	116	3,588	55	38
Utah	86	10.7	1,387	348	5,844	89	76
Vermont	85	11.4	1,102	492	7,044	107	90
Virginia	95	11.5	1,120	258	5,088	77	54
Washington	103	10.2	1,044	440	6,612	101	64
West Virginia	94	14.5	801	206	4,644	71	60
Wisconsin	95	8.5	1,616	444	6,448	101	69
Wyoming	197	8.0	1,303	315	5,568	85	51
United States, mean	100	12.5%	$1,158	$299	$5,398	82%	59%

Source: ACIR staff computations based in part on the following sources: U.S. Senate, Committee on Finance, *Major Expenditure Programs under the Jurisdiction of the Senate Committee on Finance* (April 1981); U.S. Department of Commerce, Bureau of Economic Analysis, *Survey of Current Business* (July 1981); and *1980 Census of Population and Housing*, Report PHC80-S1-1. U.S. Department of Commerce.

gram establishes national standards and uniform eligibility criteria, some states may have to provide supplements in order to retain their present high benefit levels. In this event, fiscal relief resulting from federalization will be less than complete, because states may be forced to use their own resources to maintain their programs at current levels. At the same time, federal assistance to supplement state benefits means increased costs for the federal government. In general, a national Medicaid program cannot be expected to distribute costs and benefits in the same pattern as current state spending levels.

General findings

Our review of the three major income support programs yielded some basic findings:

Relative to a uniform dollar yardstick, there are very uneven income maintenance needs across the fifty states. Returning public assistance responsibilities to the states and requiring them to adhere to a uniform national benefit standard would put very uneven burdens on states.

States have differing abilities to finance income maintenance responsibilities as indicated by differences in their fiscal capacities. It is evident that the public assistance target populations are unevenly distributed across states, and that if a nationally uniform standard is to be applied, there may be a role for the federal government to assist those states that have a disproportionate share of their population classified as needy relative to their fiscal capacity.

Both AFDC and Medicaid benefits, over which states have discretion, vary much more than benefits provided by the federal food stamp program. The distribution of federal food stamp benefits tends to offset some of the variability among states in their AFDC payments. Consequently, a return of full AFDC responsibility to the states, leaving the food stamp program at the federal level, would not dramatically increase the variation in combined benefits. Return of both programs, however, would probably result in greater disparities in benefits than now exist. This is because the food stamp program would no longer operate to even out the variations in benefits provided by AFDC alone. Currently, for example, the higher the maximum AFDC benefit for a three-person family, the lower the benefit yielded by the food stamp benefit formula.

The extreme variation in Medicaid expenditures among states means that a more uniform federal program is likely to lower benefits in some states and raise them in others. States experiencing a decline in benefits could provide supplements to federal benefits; or alternatively, the federal program itself could be geared to the higher-benefit states. In either case, the program would increase overall expenditures by the states and/or the federal government. States vary considerably in their provision of optional services and in their criteria for eligibility. These differences cause extreme variation in expenditures, especially on elderly beneficiaries.

The willingness of a state to provide public assistance, as indicated by the ratio of its income maintenance and Medicaid expenditures from its own sources to its fiscal capacity, is highly variable across states and is not related to a state's fiscal capacity. The average state spends 5.3 percent of its fiscal capacity on AFDC and Medicaid. In 1980 this percentage ranged from a low of 0.4 percent (Arizona) to a high of 18.0 percent (Washington, D.C.). This finding may result from two opposing effects: a lower capacity among the poorer states to spend their own resources may be offset by a higher federal matching rate. These effects are reversed for the richer states.

The withdrawal of the open-ended matching formula from the AFDC program could reduce benefits under this program in all states. Because the turn-back of AFDC would eliminate federal matching, all states would bear the full costs of expanding AFDC programs or reap full savings from smaller programs. As a result, states might be inhibited from maintaining real benefit levels. Furthermore, because the federal matching rate currently is preferentially high for the low-capacity states, a turn-back proposal that makes states wholly responsible for AFDC could result in greater benefit cutbacks in the low-capacity states. For example, whereas California would lose its federal matching rate of 50 percent under a swap program, Mississippi would lose a federal matching rate of 77 percent.

THE WINNERS AND LOSERS ISSUE

All three New Federalism proposals provide for a transitional period during which the federal government will make the necessary adjustments in funding in order to ensure an even distribution of the fiscal burdens among the various states. How will states fare after this transitional period has ended?

Our computer simulations of the three New Federalism plans suggest that, under any system, the unwinding of a major portion of the current federal grant system is eventually bound to leave some states relatively better off and some relatively worse off. Attention should therefore focus on whether the disparities are tolerable. A large-scale New Federalism plan that both federalizes Medicaid and turns back responsibilities for public assistance involves massive shifts of resources. The president's original proposal would eliminate by 1984 at least $54 billion of a grant system that is predicted to be worth at least $84 million by that time. In addition, it would shift responsibility for a food stamp program worth $10 to $12 billion. New responsibilities for state and local governments would total at least $46.6 billion.

The size of federal grants for AFDC and Medicaid now varies greatly among the states owing to differences in benefits, eligibility, costs, and federal matching rates. Likewise, the other grants proposed for termination under the president's plan (e.g., revenue sharing, highway, and mass transit grants) do not necessarily send more grant dollars per capita to poorer states, but because more tax revenues come from richer states, these grants do in the end favor lower-income states. While the food stamp program is technically uniform for individuals, there is wide variation in the actual flow of food stamps into the different states. Poorer states tend to have more poor people collecting food stamp benefits, so termination of the program would hurt poorer states disproportionately. The level of revenues available from increased state excise taxes would necessarily vary from state to state. So the termination of grants and food stamps, combined with increased reliance on excise taxes under the president's plan, would tend to favor richer states.

In some measure, disparities felt to be unacceptable can be corrected by the creation of permanent grants sensitive to fiscal capacity. Both Senator Durenberger and the NGA propose just such a modification. Different states will be affected differently by a plan using such grants, depending on the grant formula. No formula is likely to be able to prevent some states from winning and others from losing under a given New Federalism plan, but the formula can be adjusted to increase the flow of resources toward the poorer states.

But it is important to recognize that states that might initially appear to be losers could turn out eventually to be winners, and vice versa, depending on how prospective state savings from Medicaid are measured. If state Medicaid savings are measured according to amounts that state governments would have spent under a joint federal/state program, then states that now have extensive Medicaid coverage can be relative winners, and those with thin coverage or low state contribution shares will be losers. But if the federal government changes the structure of Medicaid benefits, the prospects for a number of states reverse. The states with extensive Medicaid coverage have residents who may lose a great deal of their benefits, and the states with narrow coverage have residents who may gain a great deal. State governments with low benefits may experience severe pressures on the operating budgets because they will not realize immediate large-dollar savings from Medicaid federalization; nevertheless, the residents of these states will gain because their medical care will be upgraded.

Who will win and who will lose, in short, cannot be accurately predicted until there is a better understanding of the full details on how Medicaid would be federalized. Our findings are based only on rough estimates that attempt to account for possible changes in medical benefits for each state.

THE LOCALITIES—A STATE OR FEDERAL RESPONSIBILITY?

Because the president's plan would terminate grants that now provide over 90 percent of direct federal aid to cities and counties (see table 4), any New Federalism plan must decide to what extent state governments should have the future responsibility for addressing local problems that up to now have been addressed by direct federal grants to local governments. If state governments are not to take over certain specific responsibilities for local finances, such as community and urban development or sewer construction, the New Federalism plan should not terminate the related federal grants to local governments. If state governments are to assume these responsibilities, then it is possible to provide only temporary protections to the affected local governments. Permanent, complete protection for local governments in each state, even if this were possible to ensure, would be tantamount to retention of the present federal

Table 4

Major Federal Grants, plus Food Stamp Coupons and Their Status under the Reagan New Federalism Proposal[a]
($ in billions, FY 1982 amounts)

Grant clusters[b]	FY 1982 $ amount[c]	Retained under New Federalism — Complete federal takeover	Eliminated under New Federalism — Grant terminated
Welfare-related component:			
1. Medicaid	$ 17.8[d]	x	
2. Food stamps	11.2[d/e]		x
3. Aid to Families with Dependent Children (AFDC)	8.1[f]		x
Swap subtotal	$37.1		
Other grants:			
1. Highway trust fund grants	8.4		
(a) Interstate related	3.9	x	
(b) Noninterstate	4.5		x
2. General revenue sharing	4.6		x
3. Assisted lower-income housing (sec. 8)	3.9[g]	x	
4. Urban mass transit	3.5		x
5. Community development block grants	3.5		x
6. Comprehensive employment training	3.0		
(a) Job corps and special populations	0.8	x	
(b) Other	2.2		x
7. Educationally deprived children	2.9	x	

Program	Amount				
8. Child nutrition and school meals	2.8			x	x
9. Social services block grant	2.4				x
10. Wastewater treatment	2.4		x		
11. Unemployment insurance and employment services	1.9			x	x
12. Low-income energy assistance	1.9	x			
13. Public housing subsidies	1.6				x
14. Rehabilitation services	0.9	x			
15. Food for women, children, and infants	0.9			x	x
16. Headstart education	0.9	x		x	x
17. Handicapped children education	0.9	x			
18. Vocational and adult education	0.7				
19. Refugee assistance	0.6	x			x
20. Airports	0.5				
21. Child support enforcement	0.5				x
22. Older Americans' services and meals	0.5	x		x	x
23. School impact (federally affected areas)	0.4	x			
24. Elementary and secondary education block	0.4	x		x	x
25. Urban development action	0.4	x			
26. Alcohol, drug abuse, and mental health block	0.4	x			
27. Cooperative education extension	0.3	x		x	x
28. Community services block	0.5				x
29. Foster care for children	0.3				x
30. Maternal and child health block grant	0.3				x
31. Work incentive for welfare recipients	0.2				x
32. Primary health care block grant	0.2				x
33. Energy conservation	0.2				x
34. Economic development assistance	0.2				x

(table continued on next page)

Table 4 (continued from previous page)
Major Federal Grants, plus Food Stamp Coupons and Their Status under the Reagan New Federalism Proposal[a]
($ in billions, FY 1982 amounts)

Grant clusters[b]	FY 1982 $ amount[c]	Retained under New Federalism	Eliminated under New Federalism
35. Child welfare services	$ 0.2		x
36. Legal services	0.2		x
37. Family planning plus preventive health block grant	0.2		x
Other grants: subtotal	$53.4	$18.6	$34.8
		(35% of subtotal)	(65% of subtotal)
Grand total	$90.5		
All grants (excludes food stamps).[h] subtotal	$79.9		

Source: ACIR: funding data from the Congressional Budget Office, unpublished, for budget authority for grants to be terminated; *The Budget of the U.S. FY 82*, Appendix, for outlays and budget authority for grants not proposed for termination.

[a]Grants listed accounted for more than 90% of total mix of budget authority and outlays for grants in FY 1982. Grants listed as retained are those present in FY 1982 that are not on the administration's "Illustrative List" of New Federalism terminations; they are not necessarily protected from budget-related terminations unrelated to the New Federalism proposal.

[b]Several clusters include a number of related grant authorizations —highways, for example.

[c]Budget authority, unless otherwise noted.

[d]Outlays including an amount based on an administration FY 1982 supplemental appropriation request.

[e]Includes coupons and a grant for state administrative costs.

[f]Outlays rather than budget authority, which is distorted by accounting changes.

[g]Outlays rather than budget authority; budget authority exceeds outlays by over fourfold, but outlays in recent years have never approached this level.

[h]Food stamp coupons excluded, but not the grant for state food

grant system with its clumsy and inflexible mechanisms of federal mandates.

All the New Federalism plans advanced thus far provide at least general protections for state and local governments. These protections include (1) an early warning system that enables state and local governments to clarify their new responsibilities; (2) a transitional phase during which federal grants can be gradually withdrawn; and (3) to protect local governments, a temporary obligation for states to replace lost federal grants to localities.

It is crucial to remember, however, that there are limits to the ability of temporary protections to shape themselves to the particular requirements of individual states and localities. These limits must be appreciated, because failure to understand them will lead to paralyzing complexity in the design of any New Federalism plan.

V

Cooperative Federalism

10

AARON WILDAVSKY

Birthday Cake Federalism

Individualism, diversity, variety in government. Pro-federalists, anti-federalists, and "picket fence" federalism. Revenue sharing. Rich states and poor states. The demarcation criterion. The fifty-first state.

Parallel play—room for states, room for national government, and room for them together—was once the neat theory of the American federal system. Under the prevailing image of the layer cake, the parts never overlapped except when constitutionally mandated. When it was observed that the parallel lines had really intermingled to become a marble instead of a layer cake, there was confusion but not consternation. As Daniel Elazar has demonstrated, cooperative federalism was the norm virtually from the outset; so there remained the good feeling that American pragmatism had apparently triumphed over arid theory. The question of what exactly to call this compound of national and state rule was, for a time, superseded by calling it good. So long as a few bands of dark were still visible against the light, there was sufficient resolution to say it was something. But as government grew from the mid-1960s, bands of marble collapsed every which way and became so crisscrossed that no one could say what was up or down or who was (simultaneously?) on top or bottom. Big government (large numbers of large programs taking a larger proportion of national income) had made the division of powers between governments unrecognizable; it was hard to tell one level apart from another or (say, with the federal government's supporting local libraries) to discern any difference in principle between them.

FRUITCAKE FEDERALISM

What kind of federal cake is this? Apparently, the layer cake and the marble cake have been succeeded by the fruitcake. Dual federalism (the layer cake) and cooperative federalism (the marble cake) now give way to "fruitcake" federalism.

At budget time it is always Christmas. The season is festive with anticipation. There are plums to be had for the picking. The closer one approaches the brandy-soaked cake, the more intoxicated one becomes with the rising fumes. One is sober enough to pick out the goodies but too drunk to notice how much one is eating. What has happened to these fruits of government spending?

If Americans do not want to get stuck in the congealed mass of this fruitcake, they might try changing the cook, but in my opinion they would be better advised to change the ingredients of their federal system to find a more individualistic cake, favoring a diversity of governments and a variety of programs.

What kind of federal cake would that be? In "birthday cake federalism," mature men and women would be allowed to choose how many candles and calories fit their self-image. Birthday cakes are individualized. Each person chooses the one he wants. Those who overeat pay the penalty. In any case, they do not eat other people's cakes and others do not eat theirs; birthdays come at different times and are celebrated in different ways. I always thought that was what federalism was supposed to be about—diversity, variety, and not a little competition.

What has happened to make the old-time glory of the American political system—its openness, its variety, its very unity in diversity—appear to be its principle defect? Before jumping to conclusions, it is well to remind ourselves of what the argument over federalism used to be about. The old argument was that federalism did not work well because it created numerous veto points that frustrated majority will: by the time the impetus for change gathered sufficient steam to mobilize support in all the necessary places, it had exhausted its reformist ardor. And even if there was policy, it had been so compromised in passage and so exhausted in administration that the confused child of implementation hardly resembled the sturdy parents of conception. The opposing position was that the modern anti-federalists mistook opportunities for obstacles. Their veto points, pro-federalists argued, were actually "multiple cracks" enhancing access to the political process. Federalism facilitated majority building out of minority interests. Federalism therefore meant more legislation, not less.

Who was right? Neither and both. There were more vetoes of proposals, but there was actually more legislation. Compromises cumulated almost always in the direction of larger size. The more big programs, it turned out, the greater the incoherence among them. Both sides had been arguing about the quantities of good legislation; both were swamped with quantities, simply.

The result is federal structure without federalism. The existence of federal structure enhances entrepreneurship in program development. Every officeholder and bureaucrat, wherever situated, is encouraged to catch up with and surpass every other. At the same time, revenue sharing to the states guarantees that the question of what states would do if they had to raise their own money does not come up. Thus federalism as a doctrine for assigning functions to areal entities, or as a process of diversification through competition, goes by the boards. Competition for the same subsidies in substantive spheres of policy—"picket fence" federalism, as it has been called—increases uniformity. In this "mishmash" that I call "fruitcake federalism" (that is, being bogged down in governmental plums and puddings), federal structure serves to multiply the offices and opportunities for increasing the quantity but not the quality of public policy.

Slowly the suspicion dawns that the old divisions may not be the new ones. As the states, the cities, and the "feds" fight over policies and payments, the people observe that they all grow larger. Perhaps what they have in common as governments is more important than what separates them. Perhaps the proper division is citizens versus government or the public versus the private sector. The growth of governments rather than the growth of *which* government thus becomes a major public issue.

The first clue to the appearance of a fruitcake federalism is the difficulty everyone has in deciding whether states, localities, or the "feds" have gained or lost power vis-à-vis each other in the era of big government. All possible answers, it turns out, are true in regard to some policies at some times but not in regard to others at other times. Can the federal government do without the states or vice versa? Not really. Will states and localities refuse federal funds? Hardly likely. Will the federal government be able to cut the states out? No. A lot of noise is created by disputes over under- or over-regulation. In the end, however, even as the participants wrestle, it proves impossible to separate them. And where they began the first round as lightweights, in the final round they are heavyweights. Perhaps, then, their relationship is not competitive but symbiotic. If they live off of one another, the pieces of the puzzle will fit together: instead of more for one being less for another, as a static cross section of time might suggest, a historical, developmental model would show that more for one at hour "x" leads to more for both at hour "y."

If evolution were accompanied by devolution, the size of problems might be reduced to an intelligible scope. And if evolution took place in the midst of competition, the politically or economically fittest might survive, leading to public approval. Instead, what you see is what there is: the "dinosaur solution" operates so that every solution increases size without simultaneously increasing the intelligence of those who design and administer programs.

My first thesis is that the size of all governments is more important than what they do. My second thesis is that citizens may be better served if we ask how to improve their choices, rather than worrying over which level of big government should monopolize a service. Students of federalism should look not only at the balance between levels of government but, more important today, at the relative proportions of the public and private sectors. If federalism is institutionalized competition among governments, increasing rather than limiting citizen choice among service providers is its contemporary key (Wildavsky 1980). By sponsoring service providers of all kinds, by separating political demand from public supply of services, competition among governments may be enhanced. When the fruitcake gives way to the birthday cake designed for individual expression, when citizen choice characterizes federalism, the taste will differ state by state—which is as it should be if we want government to adjust to individual taste rather than for people to adjust to their government.

THE TWO VIRTUES

The virtue of the central government is uniformity; its laws would be loathsome if they were to treat citizens differently depending on where they lived. The virtue of state governments is diversity; their laws would be procrustean if they repeated themselves regardless of locale. Stamping out carbon copies is something the center should do but states should not. What can we say about the conditions for these two virtues? Each one's maintaining its own style is a condition for attaining the virtue of the other. If states maintain diversity, this gives the center a stronger rationale for sticking to uniformity—its lack is being made up elsewhere. And so long as some things are done on a uniform basis, there is a stronger rationale for varying others.

Thus it is all right for the central government to limit expenditures, which facilitates a uniform rate of spending, but not for the states to do likewise as a class. For some states it is desirable to impose limits, but not for all; and even for those who do so, it is preferable that they choose different levels (higher and lower) and different modes (limits as proportions of national product or personal income, or as balanced budget requirements, etc.). By stressing diversity among states, lessons may be learned that would otherwise not be possible. By maintaining diversity, citizens may sort themselves so they live with the kind of government they want.

But the defects of revenue sharing go deeper than mere macroeconomic perversity. By divorcing expenditure from revenue, what people want is separated from what they are willing to give. Revenue sharing distorts state citizenship and state responsibility. No longer is it possible for citizens to determine what they would have wanted or to hold states accountable for what they have done with "foreign funds." In theory, revenue sharing might actually increase diversity among states, but in practice it does not. The poorer states ape the richer and the richer do more of the same; both become accustomed to larger levels of spending.

Still, some states are able to spend more than others. Since some states have oil, gas, and coal that others lack, the resource-rich are going to be better off in many ways, among them the ability to collect taxes paid, in effect, by consumers in other states. Should that be considered a problem? Some people are born beautiful, others ugly—such are the breaks. Even so, states have alternatives other than holding out the tin cup to the federal government. Resource-poor states can acquire synthetic fuel or nuclear energy plants. Yet, it will be objected, these are dirty and may be dangerous. Does the equal protection clause protect each state against unpleasantness? The answer, of course, is no; but states can choose to be poor and pleasant and people can decide whether they want to live under such circumstances.

What would happen to poor people under regimes of stronger state competition? The news is good and bad. Under the good fairy, the poor go where the jobs are and those who cannot work go where states are best able to afford high levels of welfare. The system is self-regulating: the rich support the poor, as states choose to be richer with fewer environmental amenities or poorer with a more pleasant physical environment, and people with low income are treated to what they really need most—money.

Now for the wicked fairy. The richer states may be more individualistic, in which case they may lower welfare. Poor people may be left in poor states. Should that happen, the federal government might pay poor states a subsidy for each person on welfare. Would people rather have jobs? Then there are states that provide work.

This vision of variety might not be so bad: the federal government learns to perform a narrower range of tasks better. States learn to live with widely varying styles of life. People vote with their feet for the kind of life they would like to live. In our time, perhaps that kind of active personal choice among life-styles may be as good as we can get from government.

DISTINGUISHING FEDERAL FROM STATE ACTIVITIES

Where is the philosopher's stone of federalism, the demarcation principle between central and state functions, that would rationalize a division of labor within the American federal system? The answer is: nowhere. Every effort to specify what is local and what is national, I believe, will founder on these facts of life: every national activity has its local aspects and every local activity a national perspective; any two incompatible objectives may be reconciled by a third to which they contribute, and any two that are complementary may be made contradictory in reference to their contributions to a third. It follows that no criteria of choice can be consistent in regard to all the legitimate political perspectives that may be brought to bear on them.*

The philosophical problem previews the political dilemma. Failure to specify a demarcation line suggests a lack of principle. Yet efforts to operate under such a criterion admit of so many exceptions that the cure is worse than the disease: government grows larger without any more rhyme or reason than before.

Consider the case of income security or family assistance or income maintenance, known in Reagan parlance as the "social safety net." Financed by the federal government,

*The extensive and inconclusive literature on the idea of a demarcation criterion separating science from nonscience should serve as a warning to enthusiasts.

perhaps in the Friedmanite form of a negative income tax, a floor under income would be huge. Millions more people would participate than are presently on welfare. The pressure to push benefits up would be difficult to resist. Yet these modest amounts of money could hardly cover catastrophic illness or even the everyday costs of medical care. Fattening the floor to cover medical insurance, energy, food, or whatever else is deemed to be beyond the purchasing power of the individual would raise the program totals by billions, preempting the major tax base for federal use. Why begin "supply-side" federalism by increasing the federal share?

Any knowledgeable person can make a good (though not, of course, conclusive) case for federal assumption of a favored activity. The costs of medical care could be limited, for example, by exclusive federal financing, ruling out private or state and local activity. The reason is that a lump sum, by limiting inputs into the medical system, would more effectively ration resources (see Wildavsky 1976, pp. 105–23). The relative priorities of different programs are bound to cause continuous disagreement.

What, then, should be done if one desires a federal system that stresses variety, diversity, and competition? As usual, negative knowledge comes earlier than positive—big government is antithetical to federalism because it preempts resources for the national government and because it causes virtually every activity to mix the levels of government. Variety in programs suffers as the central controllers seek as much conformity as possible.

The point I wish to pursue about positive knowledge is that we do not need what we should not have. A cognitive approach through a formula for demarcation suggests that there is some general theory, known by some particular people, to which government activity should be subject. This idea should be rejected, for that would mean there must be activities not now ensconced at the federal level that should be there. Let us turn instead to setting up conditions for social interaction most likely to produce outcomes that can retrospectively be described as diverse, varied, and competitive—i.e., federal.

THE FEDERAL GOVERNMENT AS THE FIFTY-FIRST STATE

The first thing is to reduce the federal tax take to a considerably lower proportion of national income. This reduction is permissive; it allows states room into which they can expand. (Putting tax reduction first, by the way, allows advocates of smaller government to gain control of the balanced budget issue; once taxes have been cut, the way to balance can only be through reduction of expenditure.) The second thing is to proportionately whittle down revenue sharing, block grants, and such. Current programs may be maintained but they need not be kept constant in purchasing power. The less the states are enticed into federal programs by the prospect of largesse, the more they think of what they can do with their own resources and the more varied their responses are likely to be.

The third thing is not to prejudge the issue; when you do not know what to do, why do anything? Let the states pick up what they wish; let the "feds" give up what they can. And may the best government win.

Is "interaction" a synonym for inactivity? Not necessarily. The federal government can act as the "fifty-first" state by encouraging variety through competition whenever it judges that another alternative ought to be offered to the people directly (such as competitive medical plans) or to the states (better service delivery).

To think of Washington, D.C., as the fifty-first state is to think of it as a source of diversity rather than uniformity. Why, the usual question goes, must Washington step in where states fear to tread? Because, the answer always is, a uniform response is required. Since it is diversity that is desired, however, it would be better to ask whether citizen consumers have sufficient variety from which to choose and, if not, to add rather than subtract alternatives from the menu of public policies.

Suppose no government wants to buy food stamps or some other good or service some people deem essential. Presumably the program has failed an essential political test in a democracy. Suppose some states offer certain services and others do not; will one or the other not be disadvantaged? Exactly. That is what should happen in order to achieve variety and diversity. Maybe what is really meant is that some states will end up with all the bads—the poorest people, the noxious industries—and none of the goods. In that case, I suggest the people fire their incompetent politicians and hire competent ones.

Imagine states that keep out undesirable people and industries. Other states may then pick up their jobs and their people. A policy of ecology without people, or of people without industry, or of industry without either, makes no sense. Let people sort themselves out. No telling what they will do. They might even enjoy themselves in ways as yet undiscovered.

11

MICHAEL S. JOYCE

Voluntarism and Partnership

Private initiative and the welfare state. The effects of centralism. Federalism and self-government. Faceless charitable organizations. The public-private partnership: corporate responsibility.

Someone once remarked that although Americans never invent new political ideas, they endlessly invent new applications for the old ones. There is much truth here, and much good in the phenomenon. A nation whose institutions have served it well is spared the necessity of inventing new ones. Its energies are thus freed for such other enterprises as settling a new continent, creating industries, curing disease, and exploring other planets. American society is restless and in some ways revolutionary, but it is governed by a very old political formula indeed.

It is fitting, then, that the president has organized his domestic program around concepts that have been with us for a very long time. Federalism and decentralization are at the center of the Reagan program, backed by the ideas of voluntarism, private initiative, and public-private partnerships. "Voluntarism," the president said last October, "is an essential part of our plan to give government back to the people." The idea is thus coupled with the view that both government and its trusty companion, big spending, have somehow gotten out of control. The federal government now spends vast sums on public problems, but there is little public-spiritedness in this expenditure. "The size of the federal budget is not an appropriate barometer of social conscience or charitable concern," Mr. Reagan observed in the same speech. Americans may become more charitable, he suggests, and more public spirited if their government spends less.

Such statements have not settled all the misunderstandings on the subject that have surfaced around the country in the past several months. In the United States a generation ago, the terms "voluntarism" (or, in its older form, "voluntaryism") and "private initiative" had settled meanings and did not arouse any great confusion or controversy when they were used. But this tradition of discourse has by now been disrupted, in large part by the expansion of the welfare state and its accompanying statist mentality. This unprecedented growth has taken over so many functions once considered private that many people have forgotten—or indeed, never learned—what private or voluntary initiatives are. The present administration, if I understand it correctly, seeks to restore the belief that such initiatives are possible and worthwhile and should, in a free society, be primary. The success of this bold attempt to change a nation's thinking will be critical to the prospects of self-government in the decades ahead. I need not add that where the stakes are so high, the task is bound to be difficult. I want to say a few words about these efforts and their connection with voluntarism, private initiative, and public-private partnerships because we still need a broader exchange of views on these matters than has yet taken place.

FEDERALISM

What do these ideas about philanthropy have to do with federalism?

There is a close relationship between voluntarism and private initiatives on the one hand, and vital, responsible local government on the other. The voluntary spirit, based on individuals, is best expressed at the level of government most immediate to citizens' experience; conversely, it is greatly weakened by the centralization that has taken place in government over the past decades. Viewed from the standpoint of government, a healthy voluntary sector can invigorate local government by presenting a clear and detailed picture of particular concerns, needs, and desires. People who care for themselves will also care for the commonwealth and, by implication, for the health of the state.

We must, furthermore, distinguish in discussions of this sort between the terms "federalizing" and "centralizing." The first refers to a sensible division of function, role, and authority in a complex system. Local institutions can be strong and vigorous in relation to the purposes they serve, and thus contribute to the vitality of our national partnership. Regrettably, we are all too much prisoners of the myth that people who are concerned with their local communities are "localistic" and do not care about national issues. This is certainly wrong; those who care most about their local communities are likely to care most for the welfare of the nation.

The resultant *federalizing* spirit draws upon the energies of citizens in different ways and through the mediation of different institutions. This spirit does not pit local institutions and sentiments against national concerns, but rather harnesses them for purposes at once varying and complementary.

The centralizing impulse, on the other hand, absorbs functions and energies without concern for the advantages of decentralization and diversity. Centralization shows no concern for the political division of labor. It rides roughshod over local attachments. It tends to overwhelm and even eradicate particular institutions and attachments in favor of universal claims; it does not comprehend how the particular and the universal are related and compatible. Thus centralization does not strengthen the nation by drawing on the locality, but rather tries to complete the nation by superseding the locality. The result succeeds only in killing the spirit of self-government (as we were told long ago by Tocqueville).

Both voluntarism and private initiative are federalizing in tendency because, to have any effect, they must arise from local efforts. The very terms imply that we ought to trust more in the spontaneous decisions of our citizens; they also imply that we have to make choices between what will be public and what private, what will be left to initiative and what to command, what ought to be done voluntarily and what by government program. If we acknowledge that the choice between these alternatives depends on many factors, we will be dissatisfied with centralizing solutions that give us but one answer to every question—and that one known in advance.

SELF-GOVERNMENT

Perhaps the crucial question here concerns our will and capacity to govern ourselves. This requires a certain degree of faith in the decisions reached by many citizens acting independently, in small groups, and sometimes in large organizations. If we have no such confidence in ourselves, we will want to encourage formal controls on citizens and discourage independent action. In such a case, we will not have true self-government, though we may have the appearance of it if these controls are felt to have been imposed for our "own good." There are skeptics who now say that voluntarism is a ghost from the past and that private initiatives will not solve our problems. These skeptics believe in *government* initiatives and, though they rarely say it, in ultimate reliance on compulsion. Though they often use words like "democracy," "majority rule," and "equality," they believe only in government—not in self-government. Real self-government depends on a healthy spirit of voluntarism and private initiative. Centralizers want to destroy this spirit; once they have done so, they will quickly say that there is no real alternative to what they have been proposing all along.

Let me attempt some further definitions. "Voluntarism" refers to actions by individuals inspired by a desire to do something good for their community or for their fellow citizens. The value of such actions cannot be measured in money, and they are not done for the purpose of getting money. Voluntary activity, in its best sense, is not subject to economic calculation. It is done because it needs to be done. Hence, voluntarism relies heavily on cultural and religious norms that tell us what our responsibilities are and what deeds we ought to do. When these norms decay, the works that were once motivated by the voluntary spirit must be called into being by other forces—among which the state and its associated large social service organizations come immediately to mind.

Voluntarism must play a large role in the lives of any people wishing to call themselves a community. The market does many wonderful things, but there are some things that people either do not want to pay for or do not want to be paid for doing. When they help a neighbor in distress or perform a community service, they do so because they want to help, not because they want to be paid well. The countless volunteer organizations across the country—volunteer fire departments, service clubs like the Rotary and the Lions, church groups that aid the sick and elderly—were not called into being by the profit motive. Those who participate in such organizations know that their satisfaction depends on the work's being voluntary. These tasks can be put on a cash basis, but only at a very heavy human price. A social worker cannot satisfactorily replace a good neighbor or a clergyman, and a psychiatrist is no substitute for a friend. This is one reason among others why our level of social concern cannot be measured in money—because money is less a measure of concern than a substitute for it. It is all too clear to both giver and recipient that what we will not do ourselves, we will hire someone else to do.

It thus often happens that the voluntary spirit loses much of its power when attempts are undertaken to coordinate it within large organizations. Such efforts are undertaken all the time, of course—witness our large charities, our social service organizations, or the federal government itself. All attempt to bring together scattered impulses to do good. Because this is an age of large organizations, some planning and coordination is doubtless necessary in charitable activities. But if something is gained thereby, something also is inevitably lost. When organizational logic triumphs in the economic or educational spheres, we may get efficient corporations, specialized educational institutions, and advanced research centers, to name only a few possible benefits. When this process occurs in the voluntary sphere, however, there is often a rather different result.

Organization tends to turn voluntary activities into administrative routines carried out in a regular and prescribed way. It also tends to promote a division of labor between contributors who give money and employees who deliver services. This changes the relationship between the giver and recipient, in large part because the primary parties in the transaction no longer see one another. The contributor thus becomes a faceless name on a mailing list, while the real and durable relationship is established between the representative of the organization and the person in need. Yet each occupies a role—the one stands for the organization and the other for a class of needy or disadvantaged people, or for some other category or aggregation. The first does not see individual beneficiaries, but rather whole aggregations of them; the second does not see a friend or neighbor, but rather a professional. Thus the motive to do good within an organization is routinized, and the work turned into a service for which professional remuneration is expected. Frequently this relationship is given meaning through political ideology, with the needy turned into representatives of abstract classifications like "the poor" or "the oppressed," and the professionals turned into the advanced guard of their clients. Either way, the voluntary spirit is transformed into something entirely alien to the motives out of which it originated.

Tocqueville tells us that something similar happens to the spirit of democratic citizenship when political authority is concentrated in the hands of a centralized administration. He understood the political effects of such centralization from his observations of the European states of his time. By imparting a precise regularity to social life, he observed, centralization kills the initiative of citizens, turning them into passive subjects of administration. It creates social order of a particular and limited kind, but it robs society of vitality. A strong central government can order society, but it cannot draw on society's energy. Moreover, an administrative state cannot even accomplish the tasks it assigns itself because, as Tocqueville noted, "a central power, however enlightened and wise one imagines it to be, can never alone see to all the details of the life of a great nation."

A decentralized system, on the other hand, of the kind

Tocqueville discovered in America, does not produce a neatly ordered society; but it does encourage citizens to look after the affairs of their own communities. The independent township, he said, was the "life and mainspring of American liberty"; it was "the nucleus round which the local interests, passions, rights, and duties collected and clung." Local self-government encouraged the creation of countless voluntary associations, many of which were intended to address public questions. Tocqueville admired the American system not because it was efficient in a narrow technical sense, but because of the way it drew on the democratic inclinations of citizens. Because government was close to them and was of their own making, citizens cared for it much as they cared for their own families. They rejected equally the evils of despotism and anarchy. "Those who dread the license of the mob," Tocqueville wrote, "and those who fear absolute power ought alike to desire the gradual development of provincial liberties."

It is clear that the centralization of power is deadly both to voluntarism and to the spirit of self-government. Centralization is always accompanied by bureaucracy and administration, both of which turn citizens into passive recipients of rules and regulations. In a centralized arrangement, citizens do not make the laws but merely obey them, and to this extent are no longer the real source of authority in the system. It is thus doubtful that the centralization of power is consistent with the ideals of self-government as they have been understood in the United States; we can have a centralized system—but it is highly doubtful that we can have a democracy too.

Of course, some say it makes no difference what level of government addresses our problems so long as they are addressed. Because only national action is capable of addressing these problems everywhere with certainty, we are increasingly driven into a single-minded emphasis on national solutions. But the sheer scale of these attempted solutions leads inevitably to the loss of freedom and initiative. Voluntarism is an early casualty in these efforts, but eventually the spirit of self-government is also vitiated.

For this reason alone it makes a great deal of difference at what level we address our social questions. The consequences of our actions go far beyond what can be captured by calculations of cost and efficiency. President Reagan has defended his program on grounds of cost and efficiency because, in his opinion (if not that of his critics), it will bring economic growth, greater control over government expenditures, and reductions in bureaucracy. Yet none of these gains is as important as the influence the program may have on the spirit of self-government.

The term "private initiative" means to me something different from voluntarism. It refers, I think, to a broader range of activities; it encompasses all activities in the private sphere, no matter what their motivation—profit, charity, or community service—and no matter how they are carried out, individually or organizationally. In using this term, the president is no doubt expressing his preference for the private sector over the public, and his belief that what can be done under private auspices ought not to be done by government. He has said clearly that many of the things the state has been doing can be done better, and with greater integrity, by individuals.

The idea of private initiative also means something more—that is, the call for people to "help themselves" rather than to rely on assistance from government. Here the stress is on "initiatives." People gradually lose the capacity to act on their own behalf when they know that government stands ready to intervene at the first sign of distress. Over a period of years, constant government intervention is bound to create a sense of passivity in those to whom it is directed. More to the point, people develop a natural incentive to be passive, for these benevolent props might be withdrawn at the first sign of real initiative. A diminution in government activity, by contrast, would encourage citizens to be self-governing in an individual sense, so that self-government could be strengthened in a public sense. If people would control their government, they ought not, after all, be dependent on it. Private initiative implies self-help and independence, which remain the essential conditions of freedom and responsible citizenship.

Restoring a measure of initiative and strength to private institutions is clearly a way of decentralizing power in society. Big government, as we know, creates and requires larger and fewer private institutions to deal with it. In a kind of administrative arms race, bureaucracy on the one side leads to bureaucracy on the other, because the regulations and paperwork imposed by government can be processed only by equally imposing organizations. A large, centralized government thus creates mirror images of itself in the private sector. It would be a great mistake, then, to permit the federal government, large corporations, or big foundations to coordinate the private initiatives the president wants to encourage. Such initiatives might be "private" in a technical sense, but they would still be heavily bureaucratic. This would merely continue under another name the undesirable patterns of the past.

Genuine private initiatives, then, must be simply that—initiatives, privately undertaken. They cannot be coordinated or directed by those who lay vague claims to understanding the "public interest" or the "responsibilities" of private institutions. We may have to accept the fact that such initiatives will be diverse, competitive, and irregular, rather than uniform, efficient, and smoothly coordinated. If the private sector is to be robust and creative, it cannot be expected to operate like a well-oiled machine with every part moving in harmony.

There are now many people who wish to plan and coordinate private initiatives through corporate and government councils. They entertain this wish, I assume, either because they have become habituated to looking for administrative solutions or because they see in this a way of continuing the administrative state under a different guise. Such an approach will work neither to help the truly needy nor to achieve the objectives the president is urging. His plan depends on the restoration of a true sense of initiative in the habits of individual citizens. In providing a substitute for initiative, the impulse to plan on a grandiose scale ends up killing rather than replacing that initiative.

Much valuable work will continue to be undertaken within large institutions. But I do not believe that every valuable enterprise has to fit into this mold, nor that every desirable objective has to be coordinated by the federal government, large foundations, and Fortune 500 corporations. I confess to a bias in favor of diversity and competition. If someone at the top of a foundation or corporation thinks some objective is valuable, either for his organization or for society, he ought to go out and accomplish it rather than try to enlist in advance an army of supporters to endorse it. The habit among executives of giving orders within an organization can sometimes grow into a habit of giving instructions to the whole society. Diversity and decentralization are the best antidotes to such pretensions.

THE PUBLIC-PRIVATE PARTNERSHIP

Here we come to a very fuzzy idea indeed, endorsed by people at every point on the ideological spectrum. Mr. Reagan has praised the idea, and has given it an important place on his domestic agenda. Franklin Thomas, president of the Ford Foundation, also has good things to say about it. An idea so generally approved must either be very good or very ambiguous. At the risk of creating some divisions in the ranks, I want to suggest that these two gentlemen mean very different things when they speak about "public-private partnership."

Most of the misunderstandings here have arisen in connection with discussions of "the gap"—that is, the difference between what the federal government used to spend on social services and what it will spend in the future as a result of budget reductions. Sometimes this gap is equated with great suffering and unmet human needs. Thus it has dawned on some people that programs dropped by the federal government might be picked up by private institutions, such as corporations, foundations, and charities. Private institutions would then perform functions that were once executed publicly, and this arrangement would be called a "partnership." Social welfare programs may be continued in this way under other auspices, and the political organizations that once lobbied the federal government so effectively may now turn their attention to private institutions. The danger in this, of course, is that these lobbying groups may thereby politicize private institutions to an unhealthy degree.

The belief in a public-private partnership tends to take two different practical forms: private organizations, usually corporations, are encouraged to increase their charitable donations to fill the gap, or they are hectored about their "social responsibility" as a way of urging them to assist the needy and disadvantaged. This first approach expresses a laudable impulse to help the needy through a difficult period. It was expressed very well by the vice-president of a leading corporation in charge of charitable organizations. Contemplating the impact of federal budget reductions on nonprofit organizations, he warned that "if immediate steps are not taken to stimulate private giving, voluntary organizations are not going to be able to cover the direct losses from their own budgets." He thus echoed the frequently expressed fear that many organizations formerly subsidized by government will collapse unless aid is forthcoming from other sources.

Though such concern is understandable, it is misguided in

some important ways. Much of the activity subsidized by government in recent years does not deserve to continue, no matter how it might be funded. Government supported many programs during the 1960s and 1970s that have not worked, and it supported many organizations that fulfilled no valuable social purpose. These ought not to be picked up now by the private sector. The programs should be permitted a dignified burial, and the organizations should be required to fend for themselves in the marketplace, where they will have to perform real services in order to survive. If we concede that there is a gap that has to be filled by the private sector, we acknowledge that the programs being cut have a claim on the resources of the society. If we do this, we will simply be paving the way at a future time for a replay of the mistakes made in the 1960s and 1970s. We do not in fact have a gap, but rather a public sector that by 1980 had grown much too large. The federal budget reductions now in process are not designed to transfer people to private budgets, but rather to encourage them to fend for themselves.

There are also many people who suggest, in pious tones, that corporations have a "social responsibility" to accommodate the desires of those who for so long have relied on the largesse of the federal government. They talk about the various "constituencies" of the corporation as if they were describing a political party or a federal agency, and imply that mere concern with employees, customers, or stockholders is unhealthy. They believe that corporate policy should be directed to aiding the disadvantaged. Plant locations, investment decisions, and personnel policies should, they say, reflect a concern for this "constituency." They even suggest that some representatives of this "constituency" be given positions on corporate boards in order to push businesses in this direction. This they would call a type of public-private partnership.

Obviously, such efforts ought not to receive any official encouragement. The objective of such reformers is, apparently, to divert corporations away from their main tasks of producing goods and services and earning a profit, and toward those functions more appropriate for social welfare agencies. If successful, their efforts would potentially turn the whole society into a slum, because there would be no one left to produce wealth and everyone would be needy. Perhaps those who advance such ideas are not really serious about helping the needy; instead, they may have a larger goal, which is to destroy the modern corporation. There is no case whatever for granting such political groups any influence over the decisions of corporations. If this agenda were clearly stated, no one would be taken in by it; because it is not, we ought to be careful that these ideas do not gain legitimacy under the cover of public-private partnership.

In some foundation circles, the idea of public-private partnerships is not an altogether new one. Shortly after the 1976 election, leaders of the Council on Foundations pressed the Carter administration to establish an "Advisory Committee on Private Philanthropy and Public Needs" to assume the role as "advocate for the voluntary sector." The tasks of this proposed committee were never made very clear, which is why in the end it was not given official sanction; presumably it would have identified the "public needs" that would have been addressed through the cooperation of government and philanthropic organizations. It is interesting to note that this partnership would have considered *public* needs, and perhaps along the way it would have expanded the range of government services required to accomplish this objective.

Rosalyn Carter spoke on this general subject at the 1978 conference of the Council on Foundations where she was a featured speaker. She warmly endorsed the idea of public-private partnerships and said, "I am excited about the potential of private initiative for social change." The partnerships she praised during her speech were nurtured by grants from the federal government; and when she recommended concrete steps to be taken, they involved new "government grant programs." Her idea of "partnership" thus depended on the political leadership of the federal government. Here the idea of partnership was construed to encourage the growth of the welfare state.

I mention this only to point out that there is a political background to these ideas, and that there are many people who have long been prepared to use them in a way antithetical to that intended by the Reagan administration. When the president announced last year that the ideas of voluntarism and partnership would be part of his domestic program, there already existed a network of sorts ready to turn these ideas in a different direction entirely. This is to suggest that the term "partnership" has different meanings for different people and that these meanings may be incompatible with one another.

THE AMERICAN "PARTNERSHIP"

The idea of partnership is an old one in the United States. We have for a long time spoken of the "federal partnership"—a community of many state and local governments that form a single nation. Much of the discussion at the time of the founding of our country, after all, envisioned just such a relationship. Some of the dissatisfaction with the centralizing trends of recent years is due, I believe, to a sense that this traditional kind of partnership has given way to an administrative system in which most of the partners have gradually been turned into servants.

It is the older idea of partnership, however, that seems to lie behind the president's emphasis on partnerships and private initiative. In its highest sense, his conception may be understood as a way of restoring a view of citizenship that has been eroded over the years. Thus we understand this idea too narrowly when we become overly absorbed with the various technical questions about how partnerships will be implemented, who will be partners, how much the ventures will cost, and so on. Before partnerships can exist, there must be common purposes. We are being asked, then, to think a little bit about just what these purposes are and should be. As Mr. Reagan has implied at various times, the character of our social compact itself is at issue here. The practical partnerships that we create between public and private organizations will mean very little in the end if this more fundamental partnership is in disarray.

RESPONSE

E. S. Savas: "Varieties of Collective Action"

Government is not the only mechanism for taking collective action. There are other societal institutions that can make decisions, raise money, and act for the common good—civic associations, fraternal organizations, neighborhood associations, special interest groups, professional societies, unions, religious institutions, families, and individuals. We have been acting in the last several decades as though the only mechanism that society can utilize for making collective decisions, expressing collective choices, raising money, and buying "public goods"—whatever they are—is government, and that government is somehow coextensive or coequal or congruent with society. That is not the case at all. There is a continuum of government from the federal to the state and local levels, but beyond local government there is also the neighborhood; and there are many so-called public goods where the economies of scale run out well before you expand beyond the neighborhood. An increasing number of studies show that one can do perfectly well with very localized decision-making and service-delivery mechanisms.

Recognizing the existence and utility of these other institutions is a starting point for thinking about urban policy. We can speak of a national urban policy, which is very different from a federal government urban policy. A national urban policy would take account of these other institutions—

these other kinds of societal assets—that can act to shape the quality of life in our urban centers.

The starting point for introducing or expanding diversity, variety, and competition in our collective decisions is to start thinking about the fundamental questions. What are public and private goods? What are the kinds of things that require collective action? How large does a collective have to be? Does it have to be larger than a family? Can it be smaller than a nation?

An important way to start is to look at alternative ways of performing so-called governmental functions. It becomes clear that there are many different kinds of delivery mechanisms, some of which require no role and some of which require a greater or lesser role for governments.

First, one can use government directly, as with intergovernmental contracting where governments buy and sell to each other. In Southern California, for example, there is the Contract Cities Association, a rather brisk marketplace in the supply and delivery of various kinds of public goods.

Another arrangement is franchising, where government's role is simply to authorize certain service providers and let the people buy those services directly. Bus lines and taxicabs are examples.

Grants and vouchers are additional ways of assuring the availability and supply of public services with a more modest role for government. Under a grant system, the producer is subsidized; under a voucher system, the consumer is subsidized. Both of these help change the relationships among government, the individual, and the service provider.

Voluntary associations are yet another mechanism. We find, for example, that 90 percent of all fire departments in the United States are voluntary organizations. While this does not mean that 90 percent of all firemen are volunteers, nor that 90 percent of all fires are extinguished by voluntary fire departments, it does mean that there is substantial activity by the voluntary sector in one of the most vital local services, which we need every day on an emergency basis. Even in extensively socialized polities such as Sweden and Denmark, private firms provide fire service, emergency ambulance service, and so forth.

And finally, of course, there is the marketplace for the delivery of services, with all its advantages and disadvantages. In short, there are a lot of alternative mechanisms for providing public services. We need even more of those mechanisms. We need more neighborhood-scale governmental actions, and we need to develop the ability to devolve to even more local units of government, even to special assessment districts of the kind that apparently are possible in California. We need, that is, to increase diversity, increase competition, and increase variety—for the greater good of all citizens.

VI

Judicial Federalism

12

A. E. DICK HOWARD

Judicial Federalism: The States and the Supreme Court

Court limitations on national power. *National League of Cities* **and the Tenth Amendment. Federal grants. State immunity to legal action. Federal oversight of local institutions. The Court and Congress. The values of federalism.**

Political events of the past year have riveted our attention upon issues of federalism—the distribution of powers and responsibilities between the federal government and the states. The arena for much of this debate is political—in the

councils of the president, in executive departments, in congressional committees, in the country at large. This process—it might be called "political federalism"—may cause
one to overlook another important forum for the shaping of
federalism in the United States: the courts, especially the
federal judiciary, and the process of "judicial federalism."[1]

In litigation, issues of federalism sometimes arise in the
context of constitutional interpretation, as, for example,
when the Supreme Court decides whether the power of Congress to legislate under Article I of the Constitution is limited
in any way by the Tenth Amendment (which stipulates that
powers not delegated to the federal government nor prohib-
ited to the states "are reserved to the States respectively, or
to the people"). In other instances, concerns about federalism figure in the interpretation of federal statutes—for
example, in deciding on the ambit of measures enacted by
Congress to protect civil rights.

Some have questioned whether the Court has a proper role
to play in limiting national power in the name of federalism.
Justice Holmes (1921, pp. 295–96) once declared: "I do not
think the United States would come to an end if we lost our
power to declare an act of Congress void. I do think the Union
would be imperiled if we could not make that declaration as
to the laws of the several States." More recently, such
respected legal scholars as Herbert Wechsler (1954) and
Jesse Choper (1977) have argued that questions of "states'
rights" and federalism ought to be treated essentially as
"political questions"—issues to be resolved not by the courts
but by the political process.

Such a thesis raises serious difficulties. To begin with, to
the extent that the framers of the Constitution anticipated
federal courts' having a power of judicial review, their writ-
ings (such as those of Madison in Federalist No. 39 and
Hamilton in Federalist No. 78) looked to the courts as appropriate tribunals for keeping both states and the central
government within the bounds of their respective authority.

Moreover, the argument for judicial abdication from adjudicating the limits of federal power vis-à-vis the states clashes with current realities. The thesis assumes the existence of institutional and political safeguards for the states and their institutions that no longer function as they once did. For example, the states once had generous power over legislative apportionment and the franchise. Constitutional amendments (e.g., that giving eighteen-year-olds the vote), judicial opinions (such as the Supreme Court's one-man, one-vote decisions), and acts of Congress (notably the Voting Rights Act of 1965) have changed all that.

From earliest times, issues of federalism have had a way of becoming judicial questions in cases brought before the Supreme Court. The Court's activism in cases involving federalism has ebbed and flowed. In the early decades of this century, the Court stirred continual controversy through its "dual federalism" rulings—decisions such as that in *Hammer* v. *Dagenhart* (247 U.S. 251 [1918]), which drew upon concerns about federalism to strike down a federal statute aimed at preventing interstate commerce in the products of child labor.

From about 1937 the Court took a new tack. Having been a thorn in the side of President Roosevelt and the New Dealers, the justices became markedly deferential to congressional judgments about national needs, especially where Congress invoked its commerce power to deal with the country's economic and social ills. By 1941 Justice Stone was able to remark that the Tenth Amendment was "but a truism"—that "all is retained which had not been surrendered" (*United States* v. *Darby*, 312 U.S. 100, 124 [1941]).

During the 1940s and 1950s the Supreme Court's contributions to the centralization of power were primarily passive and took the form of acquiescing in national legislation. With the full flowering of the Warren Court (notably, after Felix Frankfurter's departure from the bench in 1962), the justices came to play a more active role in reducing state and local power. Impatient with the imperfections of the body politic, the Warren Court's majority set out on the road to reform: it required that legislative and congressional apportionment be based on population, struck down the poll tax, and used the Fourteenth Amendment to impose nearly all of the guarantees of the Bill of Rights upon the states. Alexander M. Bickel (1970, p. 103) concluded that a dominant theme of the Warren years was "the centralization in national institutions of the law-giving function."

In his 1968 presidential campaign, Richard Nixon made the Supreme Court a campaign issue. Once in office, he was able to fill four vacancies on the Court. Many observers assumed that Nixon's appointees would take the Court on a more conservative course and produce decisions more sensitive to federalism and localism. It has now been almost a decade since the four Nixon appointees began serving together (Justices Powell and Rehnquist took their seats in January 1972), and Court-watchers find it hard to make generalizations about the Burger Court. In particular, there are simply too many instances of judicial activism in the past decade—the resurgence of substantive due process being a leading example—to permit easy judgments about the philosophy and direction of the present Court (see Howard 1980a). Nevertheless, the question is worth asking: to what extent has the Court in recent years appeared to concern itself with values of federalism? What evaluation may be made of the Court's record?

Several areas are worth examining: (1) limits placed upon Congress's Article I powers in the name of the Tenth Amendment (proceeding from the Court's decision in *National League of Cities* v. *Usery*), (2) decisions under section 1983 (originally part of the Ku Klux Klan Act), and (3) the Court's review of federal court orders imposing systematic remedies upon state and local institutions, such as schools and prisons.

NATIONAL LEAGUE OF CITIES **AND THE TENTH AMENDMENT**

The Supreme Court's 1976 decision in *National League of Cities* v. *Usery* jolted the assumptions of those who, ever since the "constitutional revolution" of 1937, believed that they would never see a Supreme Court opinion holding that Congress had exceeded its powers under the commerce clause. In *National League of Cities* the Court invalidated amendments to the Fair Labor Standards Act that made state and local government employees subject to the act's minimum wage and maximum hours requirement. Justice Rehnquist's majority opinion invoked the principle that Congress may not legislate so as to displace the states' ability "to structure integral operations in areas of traditional governmental functions" (426 U.S. 833, 852 [1976]).

National League of Cities struck out into uncharted territory. Justice Rehnquist's opinion gives no litmus paper test for determining which activities of state or local governments might be so integral and which functions sufficiently traditional as to trigger the protection of the Tenth Amendment. The reach of the decision is further blurred by Justice Blackmun's concurring opinion, in which he characterized the correct approach as one of balancing the magnitude of federal interest at stake against the extent of the impact made by federal regulation upon state and local interests.

In the six years that have passed since *National League of Cities,* one might have expected sequels. In fact, there has been surprisingly little gloss on the decision from the Supreme Court. Especially troublesome is the question whether limits on federalism of the kind inhering in *National League of Cities* apply when, instead of mandating state action directly, the federal government attaches conditions to federal grants. Many of the conditions attached to the grants are unexceptionable, such as requirements for reporting and auditing to ensure that grants are in fact used for the purposes intended. Other conditions, however, intrude into state and local autonomy in ways that raise serious issues of federalism. Examples include grant programs that require states to structure their administrative machinery in ways specified by federal regulations in order to qualify for aid.

An easy way out of the federalism objection would be to say that the states are not coerced, as they are free either to accept the federal program, strings and all, or simply to refuse the money. The states are free to choose. Lower federal courts, in a number of cases, have upheld conditioned federal grants upon just such an approach.[2] This reasoning, however, is simplistic. It makes constitutional limitations on congressional power illusory by permitting Congress to do indirectly what it cannot do directly. The principle is that of unconstitutional conditions. Simply because government need not create a benefit (e.g., a deduction from one's income taxes for charitable contributions), it does not follow that government may attach such conditions as it pleases to that benefit. Government may not require me, as a condition of taking the deduction, to attach an affidavit swearing that I do not believe in the principles of world communism. It is no answer to say that I have a "choice"—to file the affidavit or forego the deduction. Similarly, the constitutionality of conditions attached to federal grants is not assured simply by declaring that a state is "free" to refuse the federal money if it objects to the conditions.

At the beginning of the 1980 term, the Supreme Court was offered the opportunity to give some guidance on handling Tenth Amendment challenges directed against conditions attached to federal grants-in-aid. In *County of Los Angeles* v. *Marshall* (No. 79–1965) several states and some 1,750 local governments challenged 1976 amendments to the Federal Unemployment Tax Act (FUTA). Those amendments provide that unless a state and its political subdivisions bring their employees within the coverage of the federal unemployment compensation laws, private employers in that state will lose the tax credit they may claim under existing law. Moreover, the state will lose two kinds of federal grants, one that helps pay the costs of administering the state's unemployment compensation program, and another that assists in the administration of public employment offices (see 26 U.S.C. §§ 3301 *et seq.*).

Two federal courts of appeal had upheld the 1976 amendments, distinguishing the FUTA cases from *National League of Cities* on the ground that, as the D.C. Circuit put it, the program is "voluntary and wholly optional."[3] When viewed from the states' perspective, however, the FUTA amendments appear to have sufficient impact to trigger the kind of concern about federalism that is implicit in *National League of Cities.* Estimates of the annual cost to state and local governments resulting from lost grants range from $395 million—the federal government's figure—to as high as $2 billion, a figure suggested by expert witnesses.[4] Moreover, the displacement of state policy choices is obvious—and similar to that in *National League of Cities.*

Thus the unemployment compensation case offered the opportunity to resolve questions left unanswered by *National League of Cities.* The Supreme Court, however, refused to hear the case (449 U.S. 837 [1980]). While denials of certiorari may not be taken as indicating a ruling on the merits of the case, one may speculate whether the Court's refusal to hear *County of Los Angeles* reflects the lack of a majority on the Court to extend the principle of *National League of Cities* (which was decided, it will be recalled, by a vote of five to four).

Even more recently the justices gave evidence of their unwillingness to build on *National League of Cities.* In June 1981 the Court upheld the Surface Mining Control and Reclamation Act of 1977.[5] The act lays down performance standards regulating the restoration of land after mining to its original condition and approximate original contour. A federal district court in Virginia invalidated certain sections of the statute on, among other bases, the ground that it unduly encroached on the "traditional government function" of the state and its political subdivisions in regulating land use.[6] The Supreme Court, however, overturned the lower court's ruling and held that the Tenth Amendment challenge had to fail because there was no showing that the statute regulated the "States as States" (101 S.Ct. at 2364–69).

None of these decisions means that *National League of Cities* is moribund. It still has vitality in the context of the original litigation—namely, where the concern is with mandates addressed directly to the states as states, intruding upon their integral operations in areas of traditional governmental functions. Moreover, *National League of Cities* also serves the healthy purpose of reminding Congress that its powers over commerce, although broad, are not limitless— surely a salutary principle in a constitutional system. But the record of the five years since *National League of Cities* leads one to conclude that *National League of Cities* is more of a caveat to Congress than a serious substantive limitation on its legislative powers. Certainly one should be slow to read the record since 1976 as revealing a Court bent on using the Tenth Amendment as an active tool for achieving a balance between national and state powers.

THE DYNAMICS OF SECTION 1983

A legacy of the Reconstruction era is 42 U.S.C. § 1983 (originally part of the Ku Klux Klan Act [see Act of 20 April 1871, ch. 22, 17 Stat. 13]). It provides:

Every person who, under color of any statute, ordinance, regulation, custom, or usage, of any State or Territory, subjects or causes to be subjected, any citizen of the United States or any other person within the jurisdiction thereof to the deprivation of any rights, privileges, or immunities secured by the Constitution or Laws, shall be liable to the party injured in an action at law, suit in equity, or other proper proceedings for redress.

The statute was enacted in an effort to protect newly freed slaves against terrorism and other depredations in the South. Born of specific historical circumstances, the statute is nevertheless drafted in quite general language, yielding ample opportunity for judicial gloss.

For decades after its original enactment, the statute was little used. In the past twenty years, however, section 1983 has become the font of a remarkable flood of lawsuits. As section 1983 cases have reached the Supreme Court, concern has focused on the question of what balance should be struck between the principle of having a federal forum for the enforcement of civil and other rights and the preservation of local control of local affairs. Judge Henry J. Friendly (1973, p. 90) underscores the dilemma:

It is hard to conceive a task more appropriate for federal courts than to protect civil rights guaranteed by the Constitution against invasion by the states. Yet we also have state courts, whose judges, like those of the federal courts, must take an oath to support the Constitution and were intended to play an important role in carrying it out.

During the heyday of the Warren Court, the justices found ways to give greater reach to section 1983. Especially important was Justice Douglas's 1961 opinion in *Monroe* v. *Pape*, in which he declared that the statute's federal remedy is supplementary to state remedies and that the latter need not be first sought and refused before invoking the federal statute (365 U.S. 167, 183 [1961]). The advent of the Burger Court brought natural speculation that a more conservative majority might seek ways to rein in section 1983.

In the early 1970s the Court did indeed appear to be whittling away at the uses of section 1983. For example, the principle of noninterference may be used as grounds to prevent a federal court from giving a section 1983 plaintiff relief against state proceedings. In *Younger* v. *Harris* (1971) Justice Black, invoking the theme of "Our Federalism," laid down a policy of comity and respect for state institutions (401 U.S. 37 [1971]). Subsequent cases have extended the principle of *Younger*.[7]

The Court has found yet other ways to put limits on section 1983. One quite effective way is to hold that the underlying federal right claimed by the 1983 plaintiff does not in fact exist. Such holding ends the matter, as section 1983 does not itself create substantive rights; it is simply a remedy for federal rights existing by virtue of the Constitution or other laws. In *Paul* v. *Davis* (1976) Justice Rehnquist held that a claim that one's reputation has been injured—in that case, by the police distributing a flyer wrongly naming an individual as an "active shoplifter"—involves neither "liberty" nor "property" of a kind guaranteed by the Fourteenth Amendment's due process clause (424 U.S. 693, 712 [1976]).

Burger Court decisions such as *Paul* v. *Davis* have enraged civil libertarians. In January 1977 congressional critics of the Court's section 1983 jurisprudence introduced the Civil Rights Improvements Act, an omnibus measure aimed at overturning a number of key decisions thought objectionable.[8]

Today the criticism of the Burger Court's interpretations of section 1983 comes from a different quarter. In the past three years the Court, rather unexpectedly, seems to have veered off in a different direction from that of the early 1970s. Having appeared at one time to be bent on limiting the uses of section 1983, the Court more recently has handed down several decisions significantly expanding the opportunities to go to court under the statute.

The series of more expansive opinions began in 1978, with *Monell* v. *New York City Department of Social Services* (436 U.S. 658 [1978]). Ever since *Monroe* v. *Pape* in 1961, section 1983 had been construed as not subjecting municipalities (and states as well) to suit. Plaintiffs could sue individual officers, but if the relief sought was damages rather than an injunction, a plaintiff obviously would prefer to go after the "deep pockets"—the resources of a governmental entity. As a result of *Monell,* local governments can be sued directly under section 1983 for damages, for declaratory judgments, or for injunctive relief.

The Court continues to hold, however, that states may not be sued under section 1983 (*Quern* v. *Jordan,* 440 U.S. 332 [1979]). This does not spring from any doubt about the *power* of Congress to make states as such liable to suit, but rather from the Court's concluding that there is not sufficient evidence that Congress *intended* to override the states' traditional immunity to suit—an immunity grounded in the Eleventh Amendment.[9]

More liberalizing opinions came in 1980. In April, in *Owen* v. *City of Independence,* the Court held that municipalities being sued under section 1983 may not plead as a defense that the governmental official who was involved in the alleged wrong had acted in "good faith" (even though the official, if sued personally, can invoke that defense; 445 U.S. 622 [1980]). *Owen* may prove expensive for municipalities. Most section 1983 damage awards are probably on the order of a few thousand dollars, but Justice Powell, dissenting in *Owen,* cited an Alaskan jury verdict of almost $500,000 awarded to a policeman removed from duty without notice and an opportunity to be heard (445 U.S. at 670 n. 11). Notwithstanding Powell's concern, the Court's decision may well have been influenced by the notion that, were an officer's good-faith defense to be available to the municipality as well, many injured parties would be left with no adequate remedy. In this sense, *Owen* may be read as turning upon the Court's sense of the equities of risk distribution.

In June 1980 came perhaps the most remarkable of the Court's decisions enlarging opportunities for section 1983 suits. The statute permits suits to be brought to vindicate rights "secured by the Constitution and laws." The statute does not qualify the word "laws," but it had long been thought that, in light of the historical circumstances in which the act was first passed, the reference to "laws" was to laws protecting civil rights or rights of equality.

Maine v. *Thiboutot* overturned this conventional understanding of section 1983. In *Thiboutot*, Justice Brennan ruled that "laws" means "laws"—without qualification. Thus beneficiaries of Aid to Families with Dependent Children (AFDC) were permitted to invoke section 1983 in claiming that Maine officials had denied them benefits to which they claimed entitlement under the Social Security Act (448 U.S. 1 [1980]).

To read section 1983 as Justice Brennan did, one has to disregard the statute's origins and its historical context. Moreover, *Thiboutot*'s construction of section 1983 creates an anomaly: the remedial section (1983) is read more broadly than the comparable jurisdictional statute (28 U.S.C. § 1343), even though both sections derive from the same section of the same statute (section 1 of the Civil Rights Act of 1871). There is good evidence that the word "laws" in section 1983 should be read in symmetry with section 1343. The latter section gives federal district courts jurisdiction over civil actions claiming a deprivation, under color of state law, of rights secured (1) by the Constitution, (2) by laws "providing for equal rights," and (3) by laws protecting "civil rights, including the right to vote" (see Howard 1980b, pp. 31–32). Indeed, in 1979 the Court held that section 1343 does not give a federal district court jurisdiction to hear claims based on the Social Security Act.[10] The result is an odd one: some section 1983 claims may be brought in federal courts while others (such as the claim in *Thiboutot*) must be taken to state courts.

It will require further judicial gloss to ascertain just how far-reaching *Thiboutot* will prove to be. Dissenting in *Thiboutot*, Justice Powell foresaw that section 1983 might be invoked "whenever a person believes he has been injured by the administration of *any* federal-state cooperative program," and Powell listed twenty-eight programs—a "small sample"—that might now result in section 1983 actions.[11]

The Court may decide on ways to limit the reach of *Thiboutot.* One device would be to fashion rules of standing. Congress may attach a private remedy to a federal statute, but commonly federal laws are silent on the question whether private parties may go to court to enforce the statute. If the Court wishes to limit *Thiboutot,* it could look to standing cases in which litigants have sought unsuccessfully to have a private cause of action implied from a federal statute.[12] The Court could hold that, unless a private cause of action can be thus implied, section 1983 may not be invoked. Such an approach would permit the Court to distinguish social security claims, where the rationale for individual suits makes more sense, from claims regarding joint federal-state regulatory programs, where sound policy might give more reason not to allow private suits.

In addition to its reading of section 1983, *Thiboutot* is important for its holding that awards under the Civil Rights Attorney's Fees Awards Act of 1976 may be given to the prevailing party in a 1983 action.[13] There has been a striking rise in public interest litigation in recent years, and the public interest bar depends heavily upon the award of attorneys' fees. *Thiboutot* enlarges the opportunities for awards under the 1976 act to the same extent that the decision broadens the ambit of section 1983 itself.

FEDERAL JUDGES AND THE SUPERVISION OF LOCAL INSTITUTIONS

In 1908 the first Justice Harlan gloomily predicted that the day would come when federal courts would "supervise and control the official action of the States as if they were 'dependencies' or provinces."[14] One wonders what Harlan would think, were he alive today, of the sweeping use federal judges have made of their equity powers to oversee the operation of local institutions. The pattern was set by federal courts in the South when, in the wake of *Brown* v. *Board of Education*, judges found it necessary to draw up desegregation plans because local school boards or other authorities would not or could not do the job.

Today federal courts oversee school desegregation, promulgate detailed rules for the reform of prisons and jails, and look into the operation of a range of other public institutions, such as mental hospitals and local police departments. Judges no longer simply declare the existence of a right and hand down the traditional negative remedy telling a public official not to do something. In "public law" litigation, the judge becomes a manager. He engages outside experts, takes an active hand in the course of litigation, proposes forms of relief, and supervises the implementation of his orders (see Chayes 1976).

It is easy to understand how federal judges have come to exercise such wide-ranging powers. Once a right is found to have been violated, it is the judge's function to devise such a remedy as will best undo the harm. Often, as in many of the school cases, the judge encounters local recalcitrance. Frequently the litigation is brought on behalf of a class of people—blacks, prisoners, inmates of mental institutions— who, in the circumstances, lack political clout. Trends of recent decades, spurred by the activism of the Warren Court, have produced a litigious society, and judges, by and large, have not been slow to become reformers where the political process has not acted.

The broad-gauge use of the equity powers of the federal courts, especially where the judge becomes an administrator, has profound implications both for federalism and for democratic government. The judge who decides how jails and prisons are to be run displaces elected or appointed officials normally responsible for those institutions. With his attention focused on the suit at hand, the judge is not concerned with larger questions of balancing governmental expenditures against revenues, or of allocating public resources. If a right has been denied, the judge's job is to fashion a remedy. But no one should pretend that the fashioning of relief, especially when it involves the ongoing supervision of a governmental function, will not entail sobering costs for the normal political and democratic powers.

Some Burger Court decisions reflect concern about the extent to which federal courts have become involved in the supervision of state and local functions. A good example is Justice Rehnquist's opinion in *Rizzo* v. *Goode* (423 U.S. 362 [1976]). A federal district judge had ordered city officials in Philadelphia to submit a plan for handling citizen complaints and revising police training procedures—all in response to minority citizens' allegations of police abuses. Rehnquist saw the case as raising the question whether the district judge's order was "an unwarranted intrusion by the federal judiciary into the discretionary authority" committed to local officials by state and local law. On the basis of the record, Rehnquist concluded that the judge's order was unwarranted (423 U.S. at 366).

Rizzo represents the application of notions of comity and federalism to limit the power of a federal judge to fashion equitable remedies. Civil libertarians and others who look to federal courts as the natural forum in which to enforce federal rights view *Rizzo* with alarm (see Cox 1978; Weinberg 1977). Yet there is little sign that *Rizzo* has been especially influential. Nor does the case seem illustrative of the Burger Court's general trend in cases involving the equity powers of federal courts.

Even in school desegregation cases—the area in which there has been the most obvious use of federal judicial power to reshape local institutions—the Burger Court's decisions by and large leave ample equity powers in the hands of federal judges. In the mid-1970s the Court seemed to be throwing out signals—in school cases from Austin, Pasadena, and Dayton—that it was prepared to rein in the lower courts.[15] But more recently, in two important cases from Columbus and Dayton, the Court wrote opinions that give judges ample latitude to make findings that will support broad systematic relief.[16] Justice Rehnquist, dissenting in the Columbus case, labeled the lower court's order "as complete and dramatic a displacement of local authority by the federal judiciary as is possible in our federal system."[17] The concerns about federal intrusion that had carried the day in *Rizzo* proved unavailing to Rehnquist in *Columbus* and *Dayton.*

One might also contrast the Court's 1974 decision in *Milliken* v. *Bradley* with its 1977 decision of the same name. In the 1974 case, the Court overturned a lower court order consolidating Detroit's predominantly black urban schools with the largely white suburban school districts. The Court concluded that, as there was no finding of constitutional violations in the suburban districts, the judge could not make those districts part of the remedy (418 U.S. 717 [1974]). In the 1977 case, by contrast, the Court upheld the district court's order of compensatory or remedial education for Detroit school children who had been subjected to past acts of *de jure* segregation; the Court also approved ordering the State of Michigan to pay about half the cost of the remedial programs (433 U.S. 267 [1977]).

In sum, there are certain Burger Court opinions—notably those of Justices Rehnquist and Powell—that reflect a federalism-based concern about permitting federal courts to displace state and local control. In *Rizzo,* and in some of the school cases, this concern has prevailed. Yet when one looks at the Burger Court's record overall, it is hard to conclude that there has been much significant curbing of the use of equity powers by lower courts vis-à-vis the states and localities.

NATIONAL POWER AND LOCAL CHOICE

The essence of political freedom in a democracy is the right of choice—to make basic choices about what form of government shall exist, what shall be its powers and the limits on those powers, what functions it shall undertake. In a constitutional system, of course, the choices are not limitless. Under both the federal and state constitutions, bills of rights exist to protect fundamental rights against unrestrained majorities. The very existence of the federal system further limits choices within a state when the national government exercises powers assigned to it under the Constitution.

The Supreme Court is repeatedly called upon (though it may not express the issue this way) to weigh the values inherent in local choice about local issues—the essence of democracy at the local level—against national pursuit of national interests. Several recent Supreme Court cases illustrate how the present Court appears to be shaping the arena of local choice.

One pair of cases, both decided in April 1980, deals with the structure of local government. In *City of Mobile* v. *Bolden,* the district court, finding that no blacks had ever been elected to Mobile's city commission, ordered that the city's at-large system of electing its commissioners be abolished and replaced by a mayor and city council elected from single-member districts. Although the commission form of government has fallen out of favor with political scientists, it was once championed as a reform and is still a familiar form of government in the United States. In *Mobile* the Supreme Court reversed the district court, since there had been no showing that the commission form of government—it had existed in Mobile since 1911—had been instituted with a discriminatory purpose. Equal protection, Justice Stewart concluded, does not require proportional representation, nor does it protect any group, racial or otherwise, from electoral defeat (446 U.S. 55, 68 [1980]).

On the same day as *Mobile,* the Court decided *City of Rome* v. *United States.* Unlike *Mobile,* which involved interpretations of the Fourteenth and Fifteenth Amendments, *Rome* turned on the Voting Rights Act of 1965. As required by the statute's "preclearance" procedures, the City of Rome sought approval from the Justice Department of several changes in the structure of its municipal government, including a reduction in the number of wards and a requirement for majority rather than plurality votes to elect city commissioners. The U.S. District Court for the District of Columbia, while finding that the proposed changes were not tainted by a discriminatory purpose, held that the city had failed to carry its burden of proof that the changes would not dilute the effectiveness of the black vote in Rome.[18] The Supreme Court affirmed. Justice Marshall (who had dissented in *Mobile*) wrote for the Court in *Rome.* Even if, he said, the Fifteenth Amendment itself prohibits only purposeful discrimination, Congress's legislative powers under that amendment permit legislation that affects voting practices that have a discriminatory effect. Marshall rejected Rome's argument that, as applied in this case, the Voting Rights Act violated principles of federalism (446 U.S. 156, 173–80 [1980]). In short, the concerns about federalism that led the Court to be slow to read the Constitution expansively had less force when the Court had before it an act of Congress. In *Rome,* only Justices Powell, Rehnquist, and Stewart dissented, all on grounds of federalism.

The Court's decisions concerning land use are also instructive. In *Agins* v. *City of Tiburon* (1980) the Court turned aside a challenge by California property owners to a local ordinance that limited them to building no more than five single-family dwellings on a five-acre tract. The owners had acquired the land with a view to its development before the ordinance's adoption (447 U.S. 255 [1980]). *Agins* affirms the

Court's general willingness to respect a locality's power to use zoning to achieve legitimate ends—in this case, orderly development and the preservation of open space. The Court's disposition to defer to local judgments about zoning and land use is even more strikingly manifest in cases involving charges of "exclusionary zoning"—claims that localities have used their zoning power to fence out the poor or unwanted minorities. In several cases, the Burger Court has showed little willingness to encourage a judicial role in overseeing such local decisions (e.g., to require voter approval in referenda before federal grants could be accepted for low-income housing projects or before changes could be made in existing zoning).[19]

The Court's message in land use cases is clear: by and large, local land use policies are poor occasions for federal court intervention, and parties aggrieved by such decisions had best look to other forums for relief. A footnote in *Warth* v. *Seldin* provides a clue to the Court's philosophy. In this case, the Court used strict notions of standing to abort an attack on suburban zoning ordinances that were alleged to have the purpose and effect of excluding both racial minorities and persons of low income from the town. The footnote states (422 U.S. 490, 508 n.18 [1975]):

We also note that zoning laws and their provisions, long considered essential to effective urban planning, are peculiarly within the province of state and local legislative authorities. They are, of course, subject to judicial review in a proper case. But citizens dissatisfied with the provisions of such laws need not overlook the availability of the normal democratic process.

The principle enunciated here should be contrasted with the Court's 1981 decision in *Hodel* v. *Virginia Mining and Reclamation Ass'n, Inc.,* which upheld rigorous federal strip-mining regulations against a Tenth Amendment challenge (101 S.Ct. 2352 [1981]). In presenting the case to the Court, Virginia's attorney general argued that the regulations concerning steep-slope mining and restoration pervasively ousted the state and its political subdivisions from traditional control of land use—especially in southwestern Virginia counties, where the rugged countryside made restoration difficult. The Court upheld the federal regulations as anticipated. It is perhaps surprising, however, that not one justice, not even Powell or Rehnquist, found the Tenth Amendment argument appealing in circumstances.

In the land use cases, as in the *Mobile* and *Rome* cases, the Burger Court proves slower to use the Constitution itself to limit local options than it is to uphold congressional actions that operate to supersede local choices. Herein lies a key to the limits of the Court's willingness to give force to the values of federalism. A majority of the justices are slower to read the Fourteenth Amendment expansively in the structure-of-government and land-use cases than they are to defer to congressional perception of appropriate measures to deal with racial or other problems having a plausible national dimension. Enlarging judicial power to preempt local decisions about the structure of government or land use gives the Burger Court pause. But giving Congress ample room for legislation squares with the Court's oft-demonstrated preference that social problems be solved by Congress rather than by the Court.

Deference to congressional judgment in the handling of tough social issues has been a theme of many recent important Burger Court opinions. It is a motif that helps explain the Court's decision to uphold the Hyde amendment (which refuses to allow the use of Medicaid funds to pay for the vast majority of even therapeutic abortions), the decision to uphold racial set-asides in the Public Works Employment Act of 1977, and the decision to sustain the all-male draft registration.[20] In all three cases, congressional judgment was allowed to prevail in the face of substantial constitutional claims—arguments that the federal laws in question conflicted, respectively, with the abortion right recognized in *Roe* v. *Wade,* with the generally suspect nature of governmental classifications based on race, and with the scrutiny usually given to gender classifications. Likewise, in *Rome* and *Hodel,* concerns about federalism that might have had some force in other contexts proved unavailing as the Court deferred to the judgment of Congress.

THE VALUES OF FEDERALISM

Like any other constitutional value, federalism has many uses—some benign, some not. On the debit side of the ledger, American history reminds us of the occasions when states and localities have been simply unable to respond to national needs or, more unhappily, when state and local power have been used to repressive or discriminatory ends. It is in such instances that federal power—legislative, executive, or judicial—may be the appropriate means to achieve a worthy end or redress a wrong. After two hundred years of evolution in American polity, an argument for unfettered federalism would be as ill-considered as a case for limitless power in the central government. It is right and proper that the Supreme Court play an active role in assuring that national interests (such as that in the flow of commerce) and individual liberties (such as free speech) are protected against infringement by state and local authorities.

At the same time, federalism should not be considered as some arid proposition of political theory. Federalism has deep links with individual liberty and civic virtues. The spirit of liberty is nurtured by vigorous government at local levels, where citizens have a more direct and intimate sense of participation than is possible in larger units of government. In civic participation lies an education in rights and duties, in the art of self-government.

Further, federalism, like the separation of powers among the branches of the federal government, operates to diffuse

power. Federalism also encourages—as it reflects—pluralism. This has the practical advantage of permitting the
states to serve, in Justice Brandeis's metaphor, as laboratories, and the philosophical virtue of encouraging individual
self-expression and countering tendencies to conformity and
homogeneity.[21] Above all, federalism enhances the right of
choice—the cornerstone of political freedom.

In particular cases, as noted, federalism may have to yield
to other considerations, such as the imperatives of the Bill of
Rights or a considered judgment by Congress about a legitimate national interest. Yet it remains important that the
Supreme Court be sensitive to federalism as a value of constitutional dimension. There are several ways in which the
Court can do this. One is not to abdicate the Court's role in
establishing the substantive limits on national power. For example, to say that congressional legislation pursuant to the
Fourteenth Amendment need only meet a "rationality" test
(the standard used in *Rome*) sets up no standard of review at
all.[22] A rationality standard may be appropriate where Congress has chosen to regulate activity in the private sector
(e.g., laws governing decisions by restaurateurs as to whom
to serve), but where the statute operates to displace the most
integral decisions of local governments, the Court ought to
take a closer look.

Substantive limits on national power aside, the Court
should also show sensitivity to the values of federalism by
giving careful thought to what sort of evidence it ought
to require to conclude that Congress *intends* a statute to
operate in such a way as to override traditional state or
local prerogatives. For example, there are cases in which the
issue is whether Congress, in enforcing the Fourteenth
Amendment, intends to abrogate the states' immunity under
the Eleventh Amendment. Must Congress make clear, on the
face of the statute, its intention to subject states to suit, or
may such an intention be inferred from the statute's
legislative history? On this question the Court has not been
consistent.[23]

It is not at all unusual for the Court to resort to legislative history in interpreting a statute. But where the effect of a broad reading of a statute will be to impinge on a constitutional right or interest, or to raise a serious constitutional question, such reliance on legislative history is more dubious. It would be far healthier if the Court, before reading a statute in a way that overrides a constitutional interest as important as federalism, were to ask that Congress make explicit its intention to countenance that result. Surely this is not asking too much. It would in no way question Congress's substantive power. Instead, such a canon would discourage sloppy drafting and would make it less likely that those voting on a bill would be unaware that a statute would be impinging on traditional state interests.

In sum, by promoting citizen participation in the making of governmental decisions, by fostering civic education, and by promoting democratic choices at the local level, federalism enhances fundamental constitutional values. It is no more consistent with the constitutional scheme for the judiciary to neglect the health of federalism than for it to be unconcerned about individual liberties as such. Both values merge in maintaining a healthy American polity.

RESPONSE

W. S. Moore: "A Pessimistic Note"

In general, I am a pessimist about federalism insofar as it means a genuine, sustained revitalization of power centers in America other than the central government. I fear that President Reagan's dream of a shift of government power back to the states may be shattered. And I fear that we have crossed a point of no return in terms of the balance of power between the national government and the states.

In most cases before the Supreme Court, values of federalism tend to be swallowed up or submerged by other substantive issues. A. E. Dick Howard puts the best possible face on the Supreme Court's sensitivity to the values of federalism by emphasizing the *National League of Cities* decision and *Rizzo* v. *Goode*. The unfortunate truth is that neither of these decisions has been built upon. Neither commanded more than five votes, and of the sitting justices, only Rehnquist and Powell have expressed much sensitivity to federalist values.

In cases that ought to be categorized, at least in part, as raising issues of federalism—such as the original abortion decision, the various death penalty decisions, the aid to private education decisions, and some of the busing decisions— concerns over the impact on federalist vitality and values almost slip from view.

In cases where the impact on states is recognized more explicitly, such as those concerning immunity of government officials, the states are losing nearly all the critical tests. As

Professor Howard points out, the laws on attorneys' fees and private rights of action threaten very significantly the values of federalism.

American history has been characterized by a growth in central power. The original Federalists, after all, instituted a stronger national government than had existed under the Articles of Confederation. Much of the history of the first seventy years of our republic consists of a fight over state versus national power. The Founding Fathers clearly envisioned a much looser federal system than we now have; but national power was the clear winner in the Civil War and the Reconstruction amendments to the Constitution. Still, the noncentral powers in the federal system were far stronger after the Civil War than they are today. There was a growth in national power beginning with the progressive era in the early 1900s, but the next great surge in authority of the federal government over the states came with the New Deal. There was another great surge, as all of us know, in the 1960s and 1970s. But the distinctive feature of that latter period is that the Supreme Court became a leader in centralizing national power at the expense of the states and localities. The reapportionment cases were the most dramatic examples, but the one with perhaps the most fiscal impact on the states and localities was *Shapiro* v. *Thompson,* which outlawed state residency requirements for receiving welfare. It came right at the end of the Warren era, in 1969.

In the 1960s the Warren Court decided in 120 cases that state statutes were unconstitutional. While the Warren Court decided the most dramatic cases, the Burger Court as a whole does not have a significantly better record. In a similar period the Burger Court ruled considerably more state statutes unconstitutional than did the Warren Court. The truth is, I believe, that the prevailing conventional wisdom in this country has been hostile to federalism and its values for the last thirty years or more. There is good reason for that. Federalism, at least in its states' rights formulation, has been discredited by being massively on the wrong side of the race issue continually in American history, most recently in the 1950s and 1960s. The use of states' rights to stand in the way of civil rights did incalculable harm to genuine federalist values.

Technology reinforces the trend toward national government. The increasing speed of communication and transportation makes the world a smaller place, as does the merging of a nationwide into an international market system. An example of the weakness of the values of federalism in this country during the last three years is the fact that a majority of senators in the last Congress voted in favor of a Constitutional amendment to abolish the electoral college. Fortunately, a two-thirds majority was required, but it is revealing that only a minority of the senators in this last Congress were sensitive enough to the role of the states in this country to vote against the initiative. For more evidence, one need only look at the number of state and local institutions currently being run by federal judges. Much has been made, and properly so, of the Supreme Court's newfound deference to Congress, at least in the 1980–1981 term. But there seems to be no pulling back yet from the most intrusive feature of judicial activism: a federal judge's taking over and managing a state or local institution. A further pessimistic note is that almost half of the sitting federal judges were appointed by President Jimmy Carter. And I think it is fair to say that they were chosen with no emphasis on their sensitivity to values of federalism.

Any realistic optimism about revitalizing federal/state relations is based on one fact: Ronald Reagan was elected president. Reagan, far more than any of the other candidates in 1980, appears sensitive to the values of federalism and has selected some advisors with a like sensitivity. Equally important, Reagan's success in slowing the growth in federal spending and taxing shows a capability to accomplish what was once thought impossible. Thus we have a powerful but as yet fragile reason for optimism. The federalism successes of the Reagan administration so far have been described here as primarily part of the budget process. It is important to have a team sensitive to values of federalism making those budget choices, but I think these choices bear more on the question of what government should be doing than on what level or levels of government should be doing it. I agree with Steven Schechter that the fundamental question is what government ought to do, but the way the budget process is working out, the states could end up with more demands on their resources and less authority to make their own decisions.

We are fast coming to a time when a public philosophy of federalism should begin to be communicated to the people and to the courts. Restoring prosperity clearly has had a higher priority than restoring federalism, and the administration has been absolutely right to postpone actions that might splinter support for its economic program. But it will be very hard to make progress in restoring federalism without more than an inclination on the part of the White House to be sensitive to state and local power. We need to articulate a sound, historically based notion of federalism that is able to handle proposals like Governor Alexander's to trade Medicaid for education, and is also able to handle the energy and environmental issues that are coming before us—not the least of which is water allocation in the West.

This is still very much an uphill effort. Restoring federalism and revitalizing private efforts to provide social and other services are closely related. They are particularly related in their attempts to revitalize citizenship, dispel a sense of powerlessness and frustration, and give Americans a better chance to participate in decisions that affect their lives.

An articulated, coherent theory of federalism is absolutely necessary not only for public support, but also to sensitize the federal judiciary and to help future administrations be faithful to federalist principles. The right kinds of appointments to the Supreme Court could aid substantially in the long-term building of a revitalized public philosophy of federalism, because appellate courts more than other institutions of government need a well-articulated frame of reference in order to exercise their power and discharge their duties under our Constitution, and because Supreme Court justices have a special opportunity to articulate a philosophy of federalism.

VII

Conclusion

13

ROBERT B. HAWKINS, Jr.

Conclusion: Administrative versus Political Reform

As this book prepares to go to press in July 1982, the future of the president's New Federalism proposals is uncertain. For the moment, the momentum behind federalist reform has slowed. But it would be a mistake to see this temporary lull as a sign that the federalist idea is languishing in America. On the contrary, every indication is that federalism will persist for years to come as a central issue in American politics. For there is a growing consensus among Americans that the federal government has finally exceeded its political and administrative capabilities. In numerous areas of our lives, our representative governmental process—our

power of self-governance—has been usurped by bureaucratic fiat. Federalism will persist because its survival is intimately tied to the survival of our liberties and of our
distinctive form of government.

One hopes that the current efforts of the administration
and Congress to realign powers and programs will continue,
but the present pause in the reform process offers an opportunity to reflect on an important question: are there alternative ways in which to reform the federal system that might
bear more fruit?

REFORMING THE SYSTEM

The Reagan proposals for reforming the federal system in
one sense follow the pattern of past efforts: like previous
initiatives, they attempt to change the location and mix of
programs. In a very basic sense, this is "administrative
reform"—sending programs to another "level" of government with the hope that political reform will follow. While
this is an obvious and politically attractive choice of strategy
for a national government, it has its drawbacks. The biggest
drawback is that existing interest groups—business and
labor organizations, public interest lobbies, etc.—by and
large do not want existing power relationships changed.
Uncertainty, fear, and strong desires to keep programs at
the national level all operate to resist meaningful reform.
For example, at a recent meeting of corporate leaders in
Washington, D.C., the vice-president of a large national corporation publicly stated that he did not care whether social
programs were sent back to the states but that business was
opposed to any environmental or commercial functions'
being sent back. His reason was clear: business would rather
deal with one government than with fifty state and untold
local governments. These comments could just as easily have
been made by leaders from other sectors of our society. And

there is merit to this objection. But what it finally suggests is that a powerful coalition can be built to stop federalist reform of any kind.

Given both the potentially enormous political opposition to these administrative federalist reforms and the actual costs that such reallocations might entail, the question arises whether there is another route to effective revitalization of the federal system.

THE POLITICAL PROCESS

One possibility lies in the political process. Over the last fifty years the political process, like most governmental services, has become centralized. Political parties, of which the Founding Fathers were suspicious, now play a critical role in developing national consensus out of pluralistic society. Yet over the last thirty years parties have changed, reflecting the mobility of our society and a movement towards greater authority in the federal government. Some scholars have called for party reform that would emulate strict party discipline, such as in Great Britain. But one can argue that a much different type of party reform is needed to bring about real reform in the federal system. The influence of state and local political leaders within both parties has waned in recent times. As a result, congressmen and senators no longer feel the need to work within state party systems. This weakening of state and local influence has also been seen in Washington, where our elected representatives do not feel the real need to consult local party leaders on the development of policy and legislation. Likewise, governors, who used to have significant political authority in their parties, have lost much of that authority. Recent changes of the membership rules of the National Democratic party, putting state and local leaders back into nominating and convention processes, should be watched with interest. If state and local leaders can exert significant influence on these processes, they will also exert an important restraint on the president and Congress. To the extent that political parties can be denationalized and federalized and national political leaders can become dependent on state and local political processes, balance should return to the federal system. We would also see important constraints put on Congress. The Reagan administration might be well advised to pay more attention to reforming the Republican party as a way of creating the political means to reform congressional behavior.

The Reagan administration likewise should take into account the growing concern with its contention that local and urban affairs ought to be the proper role of state governments. While this may be theoretically correct, the political reality is that local governments have tremendous leverage in Washington and thus can make or break any type of federalist reform. This is a point stressed by Aaron Wildavsky in this volume. While the administration should not attempt to develop programs to reform local government, they nevertheless should articulate a federalist urban policy—one that seeks to develop an alternative conception of cities as limited yet viable political economies—a policy that will allow cities once again to live on their own resources rather than become fiscal junkies. The administration also should fill out its federalism by articulating a Republican neighborhood strategy as well as a competitive model of public schools. The goal should be a political vision that joins community, family, and neighborhood. Even though Republicans have always been ill at ease with "grass-roots" politics, their approach by nature dovetails with "grass-roots" processes. Nationalization of such processes through Model Cities and the Office of Economic Opportunity gave such efforts a bad name, but there are alternative approaches based on fusing real political authority with community that should be addressed by the administration.

THE BALANCED BUDGET AMENDMENT

If the federal system is to be reformed, we must again return to our fundamental foundations. At the center of those foundations is the Constitution. The Founding Fathers, if they were around today, would certainly look at today's problems as problems of constitutional design. For example, the inability of Congress to control spending would be seen as a constitutional defect requiring a constitutional change. What is ironic about federalism reform is that there is almost no discussion about the Constitution, while a constitutional amendment for a balanced budget is being considered in the Senate and has over two hundred supporters in the House of Representatives. This proposed constitutional amendment has important implications. If federal spending can be controlled, it will release resources for state and local governments. Also, a limitation on Congress would require national legislators to decide which programs should be federal and which should not. Thus the federalism issue would be forced upon Congress, and the president would be relieved from always having to raise it. By requiring three fourths of the states to ratify such an amendment, an open political process could create a new and broad-based political consensus on the limits of federal authority. It is precisely such a consensus that needs to be built if any reform is to have real meaning and political staying power.

Day-to-day practical politicians may see problems with such a strategy. For not only would it ultimately reduce in real terms the power of the national government, but it would achieve this gradually and incrementally. Its effects would not immediately be translated into dramatic action with clear political consequences. The gradual reforming of political parties, rebuilding of community-based authority, and passing of a constitutional amendment to limit spending will affect the political system slowly. But it is quite possible that fundamental changes undertaken incrementally would better realize the president's dream of returning America to the first principles of federalism. Moreover, this incremental strategy may be the only one that can finally overcome the short-term fears of the private and public sectors. Governors, local officials, and business and labor leaders may actually be more willing to undertake long-term change if it is gradual. Such change would root itself deep in the American polity, and possibly even sound the death knell of the administrative state.

VIII

Notes
References
About the Authors
Index

NOTES

6. Richard S. Williamson: "A Review of Reagan Federalism"

1. Ronald Reagan, remarks to the National League of Cities, Washington, D.C., 2 March 1981.

2. Idem, remarks before the Conservative Political Action Committee Conference, Washington, D.C., 20 March 1981.

3. Idem, remarks to the National League of Cities, Washington, D.C., 2 March 1981.

4. Idem, remarks made in the White House Briefing Room, 22 January 1981.

5. The president's nomination of Sandra Day O'Connor to the Supreme Court should be seen through the federalism prism. Judge O'Connor is on record that federal courts are not necessarily more professional and nonpolitical than state courts. She has written that federal courts ought not necessarily to be the "preferred" forum for criminal or civil cases: "It is a step in the right direction to defer to the state courts and give finality to their judgments on federal constitutional questions where a full and fair adjudication has been given in the state court."

6. Meeting between the president and forty-nine governors at the White House, 23 February 1981.

7. The so-called "iron triangle" is made up of the special interest groups, the permanent federal bureaucracy, and Capitol Hill committee staff and members. All three sides of the iron triangle have large interests in protecting the status quo and expanding federal spending and federal control in the jurisdictional areas. They gain thereby more power, more prestige, and more money. Their relationships are incestuous. Most Washington special interest lobbyists are former employees from Capitol Hill or from the departments and agencies downtown. They now are paid for their grantsmanship and lobbying on laws, regulations, and programs they helped to design. And too often political contributions to members of Congress are dominated by special interests who lobby them on programs under the member's committee jurisdiction. This iron triangle, coupled with members of Congress who sincerely oppose any devolution as harmful, comprises substantial opposition to any New Federalism efforts.

8. Margaret Hance, mayor of Phoenix, Arizona, in remarks on the "New Federalism" program of the "MacNeil-Lehrer Report," Educational Broadcasting Corporation, 9 July 1981. See also William H. Hudnut III, mayor of Indianapolis, Indiana, and president of the National League of Cities, in remarks on "The Future of State-Local Relations," annual meeting of the National Governors' Association, Atlantic City, New Jersey, 10 August 1981.

9. Charles Royer, mayor of Seattle, Washington, "Can States Handle Role Reagan Is Giving Them?" *The Washington Star*, 4 May 1981. See also an eloquent rebuttal to Mayor Royer's charges by Governor George Busbee of Georgia, "A Governor Responds: States Can Do the Job," *The Washington Star*, 25 May 1981.

10. Margaret Hance, op. cit. See this article for a discussion of the status of block grants as passed by Congress.

8. Wm. Craig Stubblebine: "Revenue Reallocation in the Federal System: Options and Prospects"

1. Any good text in public finance will address the theoretical results that have been discovered regarding fiscal federalism. Cf., for example, Musgrave and Musgrave 1980 and Oates 1972.

2. The "tax price" of some extension of a government good or service is the additional taxes an individual must pay to secure that extension.

To illustrate, let two local communities, B1 and B2, each incorporate 100 households, with the federal level therefore incorporating 200 households. Assume the taxable income of each B1 household is $20,000, for a total income tax base of $2 million in the upper-income community, and the taxable income of each B2 household is $10,000, for a total income tax base of $1 million in the lower-income community. Also assume that each local government would fund 100 units of some government service costing $100 per unit. Each of the local governments, therefore, proposes to spend $10,000. Given their respective tax bases, the proportional income tax rate would be 0.005 in B1 and 0.01 in B2, yielding a tax price in each community of $100 (0.005 • 20,000 = 0.01 • 10,000 = 100).

At the federal level, funding of $20,000 in government spending—equivalent to $10,000 in each local community—would imply a proportional income tax rate of 0.0066+ on a tax base of $3 million. The respective tax prices would be $134 for $20,000 income households (those in B1) and $67 for $10,000 income households (those in B2).

3. For the most part, state and local governments long have evidenced an appreciation for the Laffer curve with respect to specific tax rate, tax base decisions.

9. Albert J. Davis: "Fiscal Effects of New Federalism"

1. Both the administration's budget and CBO's baseline projections extend only as far as 1987. To estimate costs and revenues in succeeding years, we have extrapolated the growth rate implicit in the projections for the prior period.

2. This finding for the president's original proposal results from a view that the phaseout of the federal windfall profits tax on oil, already scheduled by law, does not constitute New Federalism—related assistance to states. Furthermore, the distribution of the oil production tax base is concentrated in only a few states. The proposed rollback in other federal excises was, on the other hand, counted as a plus for states.

12. A. E. Dick Howard: "Judicial Federalism: The States and the Supreme Court"

1. The discussion in this paper draws upon two earlier papers: Howard 1980*b* and idem (in press).

2. See, e.g., *Dupler* v. *City of Portland*, 421 F. Supp. 1314 (D. Me. 1976); *City of Macon* v. *Marshall*, 439 F. Supp. 1209 (M.D. Ga. 1977).

3. *County of Los Angeles* v. *Marshall*, 631 F. 2d 767, 769 (D.C. Cir.), *cert. denied*, 449 U.S. 837 (1980).

4. See S. Rep. No. 1265, 94th Cong., 2d Sess. (1976), p. 37 (estimates of Congressional Budget Office); petition for writ of certiorari, *County of Los Angeles* v. *Marshall,* No. 79–1965, p. 13 n.25 (estimates of petitioners' expert witnesses).

5. *Hodel* v. *Virginia Surface Mining and Reclamation Ass'n, Inc.,* 452 U.S. 264 (1981).

6. *Virginia Surface Mining & Reclamation Ass'n, Inc.* v. *Andrus,* 483 F. Supp. 425, 432–35 (W.D. Va. 1980).

7. See, e.g., *Juidice* v. *Vail,* 430 U.S. 327 (1977); *Trainor* v. *Hernandez,* 431 U.S. 434 (1977).

8. For the text of the bill (S. 35) as introduced, see 123 Cong. Rec. 557–58 (1977).

9. The Eleventh Amendment bars suits in federal courts against a state by citizens of another state and has been interpreted to bar suits by its own citizens as well.

10. *Chapman* v. *Houston Welfare Rights Org.,* 441 U.S. 600 (1979).

11. 448 U.S. at 22, 34–37 (Powell, J., dissenting).

12. See, e.g., *Cort* v. *Ash,* 422 U.S. 66 (1975); *Piper* v. *Chris-Craft Industries, Inc.,* 430 U.S. 1 (1977).

13. See P.L. 94–559, codified in 42 U.S.C. § 1988.

14. Ex parte Young, 209 U.S. 123, 175 (1908) (Harlan, J., dissenting).

15. See *Austin Indep. School Dist.* v. *United States,* 429 U.S. 990 (1976); *Pasadena City Bd. of Educ.* v. *Spangler,* 427 U.S. 424 (1976); *Dayton Bd. of Educ.* v. *Brinkman,* 433 U.S. 406 (1977).

16. See *Columbus Bd. of Educ.* v. *Penick,* 443 U.S. 449 (1979); *Dayton Bd. of Educ.* v. *Brinkman,* 443 U.S. 526 (1979).

17. 443 U.S. at 489 (Rehnquist, J., dissenting).

18. *City of Rome* v. *United States,* 472 F. Supp. 221 (D.C. 1979).

19. See *James* v. *Valtierra,* 402 U.S. 137 (1971); *City of Eastlake* v. *Forest City Enterprises, Inc.,* 426 U.S. 668 (1976).

20. See *Harris* v. *McRae,* 448 U.S. 297 (1980); *Fullilove* v. *Klutznick,* 448 U.S. 448 (1980); *Rostker* v. *Goldberg,* 453 U.S. 57 (1981).

21. See *New State Ice Co.* v. *Liebmann,* 285 U.S. 262, 311 (1932) (Brandeis, J., dissenting).

22. See *City of Rome* v. *United States,* 446 U.S. at 176–77.

23. Compare, e.g., *Employees of the Dept. of Public Health and Welfare of Missouri* v. *Department of Public Health and Welfare of Missouri,* 411 U.S. 279 (1973), with *Hutto* v. *Finney,* 437 U.S. 678 (1978).

REFERENCES

Advisory Commission on Intergovernmental Relations. 1980. *The Federal Role in the Federal System: The Dynamics of Growth. Hearings on the Federal Role*. Washington, DC: Government Printing Office.

Ayres, B. Drummond, Jr. 1981 *b*. "Georgia Governor Calls on U.S. to Assist States." *The New York Times,* 9 August.

Bickel, Alexander M. 1970. *The Supreme Court and the Idea of Progress*. New York: Harper & Row.

Broder, David. 1981. "The Governors Have Their Fingers Crossed." *The Washington Post,* 16 August.

————, and Naughtie, James M. 1981. "Governors Suggest Federal-State Responsibility Swap." *The Hartford Courant,* 10 August.

Chayes, Abram. 1976. "The Role of the Judge in Public Law Litigation." 89 *Harvard Law Review* 1281.

Choper, Jesse. 1977. "The Scope of National Power vis-à-vis the States: The Dispensability of Judicial Review." 86 *Yale Law Journal* 1552.

Cohen, Richard E. 1981. "For Spending Cuts, Only the Beginning." *National Journal,* 8 August.

Cox, Archibald. 1978. "Federalism and Individual Rights under the Burger Court." 73 *Northwestern University Law Review* 1, 18.

Davis, Albert J. 1981. "Stage Two: Revenue Return." *Intergovernmental Perspective* 7, 2 (Spring).

————, and Shannon, John. 1981. "Stage Two: Revenue Turnbacks." *Intergovernmental Perspective* 7, 2 (Spring).

Diamond, Martin. 1969. "On the Relationship of Federalism and Decentralization." In *Cooperation and Conflict: Readings in American Federalism,* ed. Daniel J. Elazar. Itasca, IL: F. E. Peacock.

Elazar, Daniel J. 1962. *The American Partnership*. Chicago, IL: University of Chicago Press.

————. 1971. "Community Self Government and the Crisis of American Politics." *Ethics,* January.

————, ed. 1969. *Cooperation and Conflict: Readings in American Federalism*. Itasca, IL: F. E. Peacock.

————. 1981. "The Rebirth of Federalism: The Future Role of the States as Polities in the Federal System." *Commonsense* 4, 1.

259

Epstein, Leon D. 1981. "Party Confederations and Political Nationalization." Paper prepared for a conference on the Articles of Confederation sponsored by the Center for the Study of Federalism, Temple
University, 31 August–2 September.

Friedman, Milton. 1981. "Good Wealth, Bad Wealth." *Newsweek,* 10 August.
Friendly, Henry J. 1973. *Federal Jurisdiction: A General View.* New York:
Columbia University Press.

General Accounting Office. 1981. *Public Assistance Benefits Vary Widely
from State to State, but Generally Exceed the Poverty Line.* Washington, DC: Government Printing Office.
Grodzins, Morton, ed. 1966. *The American System.* Chicago, IL: Rand
McNally.

Hamilton, Alexander; Madison, James; and Jay, John. 1961. *The Federalist
Papers.* No. 51. New York: New American Library edition.
Holmes, Oliver Wendell. 1921*a. Collected Legal Papers.* New York: Har-
court, Brace & Co.
———. 1921*b.* "Law and the Court." In *Collected Legal Papers.* New York:
Harcourt, Brace & Co.
Howard, A. E. Dick. 1980*a.* "The Burger Court: A Judicial Nonet Plays the
Enigma Variations." 43 *Law and Contemporary Problems* 7.
———. 1982 (in press). *Federalism and the Burger Court.* Washington, DC:
American Enterprise Institute.
———. 1980*b. I'll See You in Court.* Washington, DC: National Governors'
Association.

Musgrave, R. A., and Musgrave, P. B. 1980. *Public Finance in Theory and
Practice.* New York: McGraw-Hill.

Oates, W. E. 1972. *Fiscal Federalism.* New York: Harcourt Brace
Jovanovich.
Ostrom, Vincent. 1974. *The Intellectual Crisis of American Public Adminis-
tration.* University, AL: University of Alabama Press.

Storing, Herbert J. 1981. *What the Anti-Federalists Were For.* Chicago, IL:
University of Chicago Press.

Tocqueville, Alexis de. 1969. *Democracy in America.* Trans. George
Lawrence; ed. J. P. Mayer. Garden City, NJ: Doubleday.

Viscount, Francis, and Jordan, Fred. 1981. "Will Cities' Link to Washington
Be Cut? Views from White House Differ on Reagan's New Federal-
ism." *Nation's Cities Weekly* (National League of Cities, Washington,
DC) 4, 21 (25 May).

Wechsler, Herbert. 1954. "The Political Safeguards of Federalism: The Role of the States in the Composition and Selection of the National Government." 54 *Columbia Law Review* 543.

Weinberg, Louise. 1977. "The New Judicial Federalism." 29 *Stanford Law Review* 1191.

Wildavsky, Aaron. 1976. "Doing Better and Feeling Worse." *Daedalus,* Winter.

———. 1980. "Fruit Cakes versus Birthday Cakes: Putting Flesh on the Bare Bones of American Federalism." Paper prepared for conference on Future Forces of Federalism, held by the Advisory Commission on Intergovernmental Relations, Alexandria, Virginia, July.

Young, James. 1966. *The Washington Community.* New York: Columbia University Press.

ABOUT THE AUTHORS

LAMAR ALEXANDER, governor of Tennessee, practiced law in Knoxville before his election in 1978. Working to reduce the size of state government in conjunction with the General Assembly, he decreased the number of authorized government positions by 3,000 during the first three years of his administration.

BENJAMIN L. CARDIN is Speaker of the Maryland House of Delegates, chairman of the House Ways and Means Committee, past chairman of the State Federal Assembly of the National Conference of State Legislatures, and a member of President Reagan's Federalism Advisory Commission. His articles on tax reform have appeared in the University of Maryland's *Law Forum* and in the University of Baltimore's *Law Review.*

ALBERT J. DAVIS, senior analyst on the Taxation and Finance staff of the Advisory Commission on Intergovernmental Relations, focuses on New Federalism initiatives, state revenue sharing, and state/local fiscal status. His publications include two recent articles in *Intergovernmental Perspectives:* "Perspectives on a New Day for Federalism" and "Stage II: Revenue Turnbacks."

EUGENE EIDENBERG, director of the Democratic National Committee, in 1980 was appointed assistant to the president and secretary to the cabinet. He formerly served as deputy under secretary of the Department of Health, Education, and Welfare. The author of several articles on the U.S. Congress and the presidency, his most recent publication is *An Act of Congress.*

DANIEL J. ELAZAR, professor of political science and director of the Center for the Study of Federalism at Temple University in Philadelphia, is the editor of *Publius, The Journal of Federalism.* An authority on Jewish political theory, organization, and policy planning, his publications include *Federalism and Political Integration; Constitutionalism, Federalism, and the Post-Industrial American Polity;* and frequent contributions to the Institute's *Journal of Contemporary Studies.* He wrote the chapter on "Federalism, Governance, and Development in the Third World" in the Institute's 1978 book *The Third World: Illusions and Realities.*

ROBERT B. HAWKINS, Jr., has been president of the Sequoia Institute since it was founded in 1973 to focus on questions of U.S. federalism, self-governance, and decentralization. A former official in the California state government, Mr. Hawkins has been a fellow at both the Hoover Institution and the Woodrow Wilson International Center for Scholars. He has contributed to three previous Institute books — *No Land Is an Island* (1975), *The Politics of Planning* (1976), and *Fairmont Papers* (1981). Recently he was appointed to President Reagan's Federalism Advisory Commission and to the Advisory Commission on Intergovernmental Relations.

ALAN F. HOLMER is deputy assistant to the president for intergovernmental affairs. An attorney specializing in corporate, tax, and administrative law, from 1972 to 1978 he was administrative assistant to Senator Bob Packwood (R–Oregon), and he was active in the 1980 Reagan campaign for the presidency.

A. E. DICK HOWARD is the White Burkett Miller Professor of Law and Public Affairs at the University of Virginia. Experienced as a law clerk to Supreme Court Justice Hugo L. Black and as a lawyer in Washington, D.C., he is a member of the law faculty at the University of Virginia and headed the commission that wrote Virginia's new constitution. He is the author of a number of books and monographs, including *The Road from Runnymede: Magna Carta and Constitutionalism in America* and *Commentaries on the Constitution of Virginia.*

MICHAEL S. JOYCE, executive director of the John M. Olin Foundation in New York City, formerly held that position with the Institute for Educational Affairs, also in New York, and the Goldseker Foundation in Baltimore, Maryland. He chaired the task force on the National Endowment for the Arts and National Endowment for the Humanities for the Heritage Foundation's "Mandate for Leadership: Policy Management in a Conservative Administration," and is a member of President Reagan's Task Force on Private Sector Initiatives.

PAUL LAXALT, Republican senator from Nevada and former governor of that state, chairs President Reagan's Federalism Advisory Commission. A member of the appropriations and judiciary committees for the 96th Congress, he led Senate opposition to the common situs picketing bill in the 94th Congress and to the Panama treaties in the 95th.

JOHN McCLAUGHRY is senior policy adviser in the White House Office of Policy Development and was in charge of the Reagan administration's transition team for the White House Office of Intergovernmental Relations. He has been a member of the Vermont House of Representatives, a legislative aide in the U.S. Senate, and a member of the National Commission on Neighborhoods. His published works include a chapter on neighborhood revitalization in the Hoover Institution publication *The United States in the 1980's*, and on state land use controls in the Institute's 1975 book *No Land Is an Island.*

W. S. MOORE is director of legal policy studies at the American Enterprise Institute. His work in policy research and legislative analysis of constitutional issues led to his responsibility for developing AEI's Center for the Study of Government Regulation. His most recent publication is *The Constitution and the Budget.*

E. S. SAVAS is assistant secretary for policy development and research in the Department of Housing and Urban Development and principal adviser to the secretary of HUD on departmental policy, program evaluation, and research. A former director of the Center for Government Studies and professor of public systems management at the Graduate School of Business, Columbia University, he is the author of many articles and of five books, the most recent including *Alternatives for Delivering Public Services: Improved Performance* and *Computer Control of Industrial Processes.*

WILLIAM A. SCHAMBRA is assistant director of constitutional studies at the American Enterprise Institute. He coedited the AEI publications *How Democratic Is the Constitution?* and *How Capitalistic Is the Constitution?*, and is editing a collection of essays by the late Martin Diamond.

STEPHEN L. SCHECHTER, associate professor of political science at Russell Sage College, Troy, New York, is a fellow of the Center for the Study of Federalism at Temple University, Philadelphia, codirector of the Workshop on American Federalism, and one of the founders of the Joint Center for Federal and Regional Studies and the International Association of Centers for Federal Studies in Basle, Switzerland. The author of a number of articles on the theory and practice of U.S. federalism, he is also annual review editor of *Publius: The Journal of Federalism.*

WM. CRAIG STUBBLEBINE, Von Tobel Professor of Political Science and director of the Center for the Study of Law Structures at the Claremont McKenna College and Graduate School, serves as vice-president of the Western Tax Association, president of Laws at

Work, director and senior associate of Public Associates Incorporated, and founding director of the National Tax Limitation Committee. He chairs the national committee that drafted the proposed Federal Spending Limitation Amendment before Congress in 1982, and is the author of articles on property rights and finance.

DAVID B. SWOAP is under secretary of the Department of Health and Human Services and is directly responsible for coordinating regional and field activities and federal/state relations. He has served as legislative director for Senator William Armstrong (R—Colorado), as a staff member of the Senate Committee on Finance, and as a senior research associate responsible for health and welfare legislation with the Republican Study Committee of the House of Representatives.

MURRAY L. WEIDENBAUM chairs the Council of Economic Advisers and is currently on leave of absence from Washington University in St. Louis, Missouri. He is a former assistant secretary to the Treasury for economic policy, and before joining the Reagan administration he was coeditor of the magazine *Regulation,* a member of the board of economists of *Time* magazine, and a columnist for the *Los Angeles Times* syndicate and *Washington Report.* His publications include the chapter on "The Contrast between Government and Business Planning" in the Institute's 1976 book *The Politics of Planning,* and his two recent books — *The Future of Business Regulation* and *Business, Government, and the Public* — appeared in 1980 and 1981.

F. CLIFTON WHITE, a public affairs counselor, is president of F. Clifton White and Associates, Inc., in Greenwich, Connecticut, and an affiliate of the Martin Ryan Haley Company in Washington, D.C. An adviser on governments and politics, he was credited in 1964 with securing the Republican nomination for Barry Goldwater. He was a member of the President's Advisory Commission on Intergovernmental Relations during the 1976—1978 period.

AARON WILDAVSKY, professor of political science at the University of California, Berkeley, was a member of the team named by the National Tax Limitation Committee to draft the proposed constitutional amendment to limit government spending. His recent publications include *How to Limit Government Spending,* the chapter on "Budgets as Compromises among Social Orders" in the Institute's 1982 publication *The Federal Budget: Economics and Politics* and, with Hugh Heclo, *the Private Government of Public Money.*

RICHARD S. WILLIAMSON is assistant to the president for intergovernmental affairs, the liaison between the White House and state and local officials. He is a former legislative counsel and administrative assistant to Congressman Philip M. Crane (R—Illinois), and is coeditor with Senator Paul Laxalt of *A Changing America: Conservatives View the 80's from the United States Senate.*

INDEX

THE CRISIS IN SOCIAL SECURITY: PROBLEMS AND PROSPECTS
Edited by Michael J. Boskin
> $6.95. 222 pages. Publication date: April 1977; 2d ed. rev., 1978, 1979
> ISBN 0–917616–16–2/1977; 0–917616–25–1/1978
> Library of Congress No. 77–72542

Contributors: Michael J. Boskin, George F. Break, Rita Ricardo Campbell, Edward Cowan, Martin S. Feldstein, Milton Friedman, Douglas R. Munro, Donald O. Parsons, Carl V. Patton, Joseph A. Pechman, Sherwin Rosen, W. Kip Viscusi, Richard J. Zeckhauser

THE ECONOMY IN THE 1980s: A PROGRAM FOR
GROWTH AND STABILITY
Edited by Michael J. Boskin
> $7.95 (paper). 462 pages. Publication date: June 1980
> ISBN 0–917616–39–1
> Library of Congress No. 80–80647
> $17.95 (cloth). 462 pages. Publication date: August 1980
> ISBN 0–87855–399–1. Available through Transaction Books, Rutgers–The State University, New Brunswick, NJ 08903

Contributors: Michael J. Boskin, George F. Break, John T. Cuddington, Patricia Drury, Alain Enthoven, Laurence J. Kotlikoff, Ronald I. McKinnon, John H. Pencavel, Henry S. Rowen, John L. Scadding, John B. Shoven, James L. Sweeney, David J. Teece

EMERGING COALITIONS IN AMERICAN POLITICS
Edited by Seymour Martin Lipset
> $6.95. 524 pages. Publication date: June 1978
> ISBN 0–917616–22–7
> Library of Congress No. 78–53414

Contributors: Jack Bass, David S. Broder, Jerome M. Clubb, Edward H. Crane III, Walter De Vries, Andrew M. Greeley, S. I. Hayakawa, Tom Hayden, Milton Himmelfarb, Richard Jensen, Paul Kleppner, Everett Carll Ladd, Jr., Seymour Martin Lipset, Robert A. Nisbet, Michael Novak, Gary R. Orren, Nelson W. Polsby, Joseph L. Rauh, Jr., Stanley Rothman, William A. Rusher, William Schneider, Jesse M. Unruh, Ben J. Wattenberg

THE FAIRMONT PAPERS: BLACK ALTERNATIVES CONFERENCE,
SAN FRANCISCO, DECEMBER 1980
> $5.95. 174 pages. Publication date: March 1981
> ISBN 0–917616–42–1
> Library of Congress No. 81–80735

Contributors: Bernard E. Anderson, Thomas L. Berkley, Michael J. Boskin, Randolph W. Bromery, Tony Brown, Milton Friedman, Wendell Wilkie Gunn, Charles V. Hamilton, Robert B. Hawkins, Jr., Maria Lucia Johnson, Martin L. Kilson, James Lorenz, Henry Lucas, Jr., Edwin Meese III, Clarence M. Pendleton, Jr., Dan J. Smith, Thomas Sowell, Chuck Stone, Percy E. Sutton, Clarence Thomas, Gloria E. A. Toote, Walter E. Williams, Oscar Wright

THE FEDERAL BUDGET: ECONOMICS AND POLITICS
Edited by Aaron Wildavsky and Michael J. Boskin
> $8.95 (paper). 411 pages. Publication date: July 1982
> ISBN 0–917616–48–0
> Library of Congress No. 81–86378
> $19.95 (cloth). 411 pages. Publication date: July 1982
> ISBN 0–917616–49–9

Contributors: James W. Abellera, Marcy E. Avrin, Michael J. Boskin, George F. Break, Alain C. Enthoven, Robert W. Hartman, Herschel Kanter, Melvyn B. Krauss, Roger P. Labrie, Arnold J. Meltsner, Rudolph G. Penner, Alvin Rabushka, Robert D. Reischauer, Laurence S. Seidman, Aaron Wildavsky

FEDERAL TAX REFORM: MYTHS AND REALITIES
Edited by Michael J. Boskin
> $5.95. 270 pages. Publication date: September 1978
> ISBN 0–917616–32–4
> Library of Congress No. 78–61661

Contributors: Robert J. Barro, Michael J. Boskin, George F. Break, Jerry R. Green, Laurence J. Kotlikoff, Mordecai Kurz, Peter Mieszkowski, John B. Shoven, Paul J. Taubman, John Whalley

GOVERNMENT CREDIT ALLOCATION: WHERE DO WE GO
FROM HERE?
> $4.95. 208 pages. Publication date: November 1975
> ISBN 0–917616–02–2
> Library of Congress No. 75–32951

Contributors: George J. Benston, Karl Brunner, Dwight M. Jaffe, Omotunde E. G. Johnson, Edward J. Kane, Thomas Mayer, Allan H. Meltzer

NATIONAL SECURITY IN THE 1980s: FROM
WEAKNESS TO STRENGTH
Edited by W. Scott Thompson
> $8.95 (paper). 524 pages. Publication date: May 1980
> ISBN 0–917616–38–3
> Library of Congress No. 80–80648
> $19.95 (cloth). 524 pages. Publication date: August 1980
> ISBN 0–87855–412–2. Available through Transaction Books, Rutgers–The State University, New Brunswick, NJ 08903

Contributors: Kenneth L. Adelman, Richard R. Burt, Miles M. Costick, Robert F. Ellsworth, Fred Charles Iklé, Geoffrey T. H. Kemp, Edward N. Luttwak, Charles Burton Marshall, Paul H. Nitze, Sam Nunn, Henry S. Rowen, Leonard Sullivan, Jr., W. Scott Thompson, William R. Van Cleave, Francis J. West, Jr., Albert Wohlstetter, Elmo R. Zumwalt, Jr.

NEW DIRECTIONS IN PUBLIC HEALTH CARE: A PRESCRIPTION
FOR THE 1980s
Edited by Cottom M. Lindsay
$6.95 (paper). 279 pages. Publication date: May 1976;
3d ed. rev., 1980
ISBN 0−917616−37−5
Library of Congress No. 79−92868
$16.95 (cloth). 290 pages. Publication date: April 1980
ISBN 0−87855−394−0. Available through Transaction Books,
Rutgers−The State University, New Brunswick, NJ 08903
Contributors: Alain Enthoven, W. Philip Gramm, Leon R. Kass, Keith B.
Leffler, Cotton M. Lindsay, Jack A. Meyer, Charles E. Phelps,
Thomas C. Schelling, Harry Schwartz, Arthur Seldon, David A.
Stockman, Lewis Thomas

OPTIONS FOR U.S. ENERGY POLICY
$6.95. 317 pages. Publication date: September 1977
ISBN 0−917616−20−0
Library of Congress No. 77−89094
Contributors: Albert Carnesale, Stanley M. Greenfield, Fred S. Hoffman,
Edward J. Mitchell, William R. Moffat, Richard Nehring, Robert S.
Pindyck, Norman C. Rasmussen, David J. Rose, Henry S. Rowen,
James L. Sweeney, Arthur W. Wright

PARENTS, TEACHERS, AND CHILDREN: PROSPECTS FOR CHOICE
IN AMERICAN EDUCATION
$5.95. 336 pages. Publication date: June 1977
ISBN 0−917616−18−9
Library of Congress No. 77−79164
Contributors: James S. Coleman, John E. Coons, William H. Cornog, Denis
P. Doyle, E. Babette Edwards, Nathan Glazer, Andrew M. Greeley,
R. Kent Greenawalt, Marvin Lazerson, William C. McCready,
Michael Novak, John P. O'Dwyer, Robert Singleton, Thomas Sowell,
Stephen D. Sugarman, Richard E. Wagner

PARTY COALITIONS IN THE 1980s
Edited by Seymour Martin Lipset
$8.95 (paper). 480 pages. Publication date: November 1981
ISBN 0−917616−43−X
Library of Congress No. 81−83095
$19.95 (cloth). 480 pages. Publication date: November 1981
ISBN 0−917616−45−6
Contributors: John B. Anderson, David S. Broder, Walter Dean Burnham,
Patrick Caddell, Jerome M. Clubb, E. J. Dionne, Jr., Alan M. Fisher,
Michael Harrington, S. I. Hayakawa, Richard Jensen, Paul Kleppner,
Everett Carll Ladd, Seymour Martin Lipset, Arthur D. Miller, Howard
Phillips, Norman Podhoretz, Nelson W. Polsby, Richard M. Scammon,
William Schneider, Martin P. Wattenberg, Richard B. Wirthlin

POLITICS AND THE OVAL OFFICE: TOWARDS
PRESIDENTIAL GOVERNANCE
Edited by Arnold J. Meltsner
$7.95 (paper). 332 pages. Publication date: February 1981
ISBN 0−917616−40−5
Library of Congress No. 80−69617
$18.95 (cloth). 332 pages. Publication date: April 1981
ISBN 0−87855−428−9. Available through Transaction Books,
Rutgers−The State University, New Brunswick, NJ 08903
Contributors: Richard K. Betts, Jack Citrin, Eric L. Davis, Robert M.
Entman, Robert E. Hall, Hugh Heclo, Everett Carll Ladd, Jr., Arnold
J. Meltsner, Charles Peters, Robert S. Pindyck, Francis E. Rourke,
Martin M. Shapiro, Peter L. Szanton

THE POLITICS OF PLANNING: A REVIEW AND CRITIQUE OF
CENTRALIZED ECONOMIC PLANNING
Edited by A. Lawrence Chickering
$5.95. 367 pages. Publication date: March 1976
ISBN 0−917616−05−7
Library of Congress No. 76−7714
Contributors: B. Bruce-Briggs, James Buchanan, A. Lawrence Chickering,
Ralph Harris, Robert B. Hawkins, Jr., George W. Hilton, Richard
Mancke, Richard Muth, Vincent Ostrom, Svetozar Pejovich, Myron
Sharpe, John Sheahan, Herbert Stein, Gordon Tullock, Ernest van
den Haag, Paul H. Weaver, Murray L. Weidenbaum, Hans
Willgerodt, Peter P. Witonski

PUBLIC EMPLOYEE UNIONS: A STUDY OF THE CRISIS IN
PUBLIC SECTOR LABOR RELATIONS
Edited by A. Lawrence Chickering.
$6.95. 251 pages. Publication date: June 1976; 2d ed. rev., 1977
ISBN 0−917616−24−3
Library of Congress No. 76−18409
Contributors: A. Lawrence Chickering, Jack D. Douglas, Raymond D.
Horton, Theodore W. Kheel, David Lewin, Seymour Martin Lipset,
Harvey C. Mansfield, Jr., George Meany, Robert A. Nisbet, Daniel
Orr, A. H. Raskin, Wes Uhlman, Harry H. Wellington, Charles B.
Wheeler, Jr., Ralph K. Winter, Jr., Jerry Wurf

REGULATING BUSINESS: THE SEARCH FOR AN OPTIMUM
Edited by Donald P. Jacobs
$6.95. 261 pages. Publication date: April 1978
ISBN 0−917616−27−8
Library of Congress No. 78−50678
Contributors: Chris Argyris, A. Lawrence Chickering, Penny Hollander
Feldman, Richard H. Holton, Donald P. Jacobs, Alfred E. Kahn, Paul
W. MacAvoy, Almarin Phillips, V. Kerry Smith, Paul H. Weaver,
Richard J. Zeckhauser

SOCIAL REGULATION: STRATEGIES FOR REFORM
Edited by Eugene Bardach and Robert A. Kagan
$8.95 (paper). 420 pages. Publication date: March 1982
ISBN 0–917616–46–4
Library of Congress No. 81–85279
$19.95 (cloth). 420 pages. Publication date: March 1982
ISBN 0–917616–47–2
Contributors: Lawrence S. Bacow, Eugene Bardach, Paul Danaceau, George
C. Eads, Joseph Ferreira, Jr., Thomas P. Grumbly, William R.
Havender, Robert A. Kagan, Michael H. Levin, Michael O'Hare,
Stuart M. Pape, Timothy J. Sullivan

TARIFFS, QUOTAS, AND TRADE: THE POLITICS
OF PROTECTIONISM
$7.95. 332 pages. Publication date: February 1979
ISBN 0–917616–34–0
Library of Congress No. 78–66267
Contributors: Walter Adams, Ryan C. Amacher, Sven W. Arndt, Malcolm D.
Bale, John T. Cuddington, Alan V. Deardorff, Joel B. Dirlam, Roger
D. Hansen, H. Robert Heller, D. Gale Johnson, Robert O. Keohane,
Michael W. Keran, Rachel McCulloch, Ronald I. McKinnon, Gordon
W. Smith, Robert M. Stern, Richard James Sweeney, Robert D.
Tollison, Thomas D. Willett

THE THIRD WORLD: PREMISES OF U.S. POLICY
Edited by W. Scott Thompson
$7.95. 334 pages. Publication date: November 1978
ISBN 0–917616–30–8
Library of Congress No. 78–67593
Contributors: Dennis Austin, Peter T. Bauer, Max Beloff, Richard E. Bissell,
Daniel J. Elazar, S. E. Finer, Allan E. Goodman, Nathaniel H. Leff,
Seymour Martin Lipset, Edward N. Luttwak, Daniel Pipes, Wilson E.
Schmidt, Anthony Smith, W. Scott Thompson, Basil S. Yamey

UNION CONTROL OF PENSION FUNDS: WILL THE NORTH
RISE AGAIN?
$2.00. 41 pages. Publication date: July 1979
ISBN 0–917616–36–7
Library of Congress No. 78–66581
Author: George J. Borjas

WATER BANKING: HOW TO STOP WASTING
AGRICULTURAL WATER
$2.00. 56 pages. Publication date: January 1978
ISBN 0–917616–26–X
Library of Congress No. 78–50766
Authors: Sotirios Angelides, Eugene Bardach

WHAT'S NEWS: THE MEDIA IN AMERICAN SOCIETY
Edited by Elie Abel

> $7.95 (paper). 296 pages. Publication date: June 1981
> ISBN 0–917616–41–3
> Library of Congress No. 81–81414
> $18.95 (cloth). 300 pages. Publication date: August 1981
> ISBN 0–87855–448–3. Available through Transaction Books,
> Rutgers–The State University, New Brunswick, NJ 08903

Contributors: Elie Abel, Robert L. Bartley, George Comstock, Edward Jay
> Epstein, William A. Henry III, John L. Hulteng, Theodore Peterson,
> Ithiel de Sola Pool, William E. Porter, Michael Jay Robinson, James
> N. Rosse, Benno C. Schmidt, Jr.

THE WORLD CRISIS IN SOCIAL SECURITY
Edited by Jean-Jacques Rosa

> $9.95. 245 pages. Publication date: May 1982
> ISBN 0–917616–44–8

Contributors: Onorato Castellino, A. Lawrence Chickering, Richard
> Hemming, Martin C. Janssen, Karl Heinz Juttemeier, John A. Kay,
> Heinz H. Muller, Hans-Georg Petersen, Jean-Jacques Rosa, Sherwin
> Rosen, Ingemar Stahl, Noriyuki Takayama

JOURNAL OF CONTEMPORARY STUDIES

> $15/one year, $25/two years, $4/single issue. For delivery outside the
> United States, add $2/year surface mail, $10/year airmail

A quarterly journal that is a forum for lively and readable studies on foreign
> and domestic public policy issues. Directed toward general readers as
> well as policymakers and academics, emphasizing debate and
> controversy, it publishes the highest quality articles without regard
> to political or ideological bent.

The Journal of Contemporary Studies is a member of the Transaction
Periodicals Consortium. Institute for Contemporary Studies books
are distributed by Transaction Books, Rutgers University, New
Brunswick, NJ 08903.